The Sin of Lying

The Sin of Lying

B. E. Echols

The Sin of Lying

by B. E. Echols

©Copyright 1946, 1963 by B. E. Echols
Third edition copyright 1999 by Word Aflame Press
Hazelwood, MO 63042-2299
Reprint History: 2001
Cover design by Paul Povolni

All Scripture quotations in this book are from the King James Version of the Bible unless otherwise identified.

Printed in United States of America.

Printed by

WORD AFLAME®PRESS
8855 DUNN ROAD
HAZELWOOD, MO 63042-2299

Library of Congress Cataloging-in-Publication Data

Echols, B. E.
    The sin of lying / B. E. Echols. — 3rd ed.
        p.   cm.
    ISBN 1-56722-235-8
    1. Truthfulness and falsehood—Religious aspects—Christianity.
I. Title.
BV4627.F3E24   1999
241'.673—dc21   99-38438
                                                                 CIP

I prayerfully and sincerely dedicate this book,

in the name of Jesus Christ, to all truth-loving people—

who love the whole truth and nothing but the truth, so help

them God! Yea, I dedicate it to all those Christians who are

concerned about doing something to help rescue people from all

their untruthful ways and lead them into that God-given expe-

rience of John 16:13 and Romans 9:1, which delivers men and

women, boys and girls, from the soul-damning sin of lying

(Revelation 21:8; Psalm 101:7), and helps them to become

one hundred percent truthful. Praise the Lord!

Contents

Preface

Preface to the First Edition

I present this book on *The Sin of Lying* to my many friends, church folk of our faith, and the public in general, after having made an extensive study and research of this damnable sin and also after having given lectures and Bible lessons in many Northern and Southern states concerning almost everything presented. Seeing it proved to be one of the most awakening and heart-searching messages God ever gave me, I have felt urged to put it into book form so it might be placed in the hands of people who might never have the opportunity to hear teaching upon this subject.

It takes the Holy Ghost to reveal the sinfulness of sin, and when it is thus revealed, things are made to appear to the natural man as though one could never be saved; but that is the outlook of the human mind without taking God into consideration. After listening to our Lord's teaching on some important matters, the apostles once asked Him, "Who then can be saved?" Jesus answered them by saying, "The things which are impossible with men are possible with God." [See Luke 18:26-27.] Just as certain as the Holy Ghost reveals the sinfulness of sin, it also provides the means and power by which one can rid himself of sin, of any nature, and keep himself from becoming contaminated with it again. (See Romans 8:2-4; Acts 1:8.)

Your study of this sin will likely bring you to the place where you will quake and tremble in your mind and spirit, if not in the flesh as Moses did when God appeared on Mount Sinai, but it is good for us to be stripped of all our self-righteous garments occasionally and be made to see our human frailty and our need of God. As the old hymn goes, "I need Thee, O I need Thee. Every hour I need Thee." May the reading of this book give you the hymn writer's vision of your need of God.

B. E. Echols, author

Preface to the Second Edition

The first edition of this book, consisting of five thousand copies, has had worldwide circulation and has proven to be one of the most heart-searching and soul-stirring messages the Lord ever blessed me to write. I had thought I would not reprint it, but orders keep coming for them and finally a sister with a national radio program wrote that she would like to have another thousand of them. So I am revising, adding a few more points on the forms of lying, and reprinting the book otherwise as it was in the first edition. May God continue to use it to His glory and bless the hearts of all those who will read this second edition, is my wish and prayer.

B. E. Echols, author

Editor's Preface to the Third Edition

This edition has been published with the permission of the B. E. Echols family. It was placed on computer and prepared for publication by Rich Lyons, pastor of the United Pentecostal Church in Marshall, Texas, where B. E. Echols resided until his death. It is essentially the same as the second edition. Punctuation, capitalization, Scripture citation, spelling, diction, and grammar have been edited to conform to current Word Aflame Press house rules. A few editor's comments have been inserted in brackets, and a few missing Scripture citations have been supplied in brackets. Several paragraphs and sentences have been omitted because they were not directly relevant to the subject of lying and could therefore be confusing in the context. These omissions have been noted by ellipses (. . .). Otherwise, the content of the book remains the same. Within quotations of Scripture, ellipses and bracketed comments are the author's.

Endorsements

This book, *The Sin of Lying*, is certainly a commendable work, and I have never read anything like it. It should be in every home because of the truth set forth in its pages. May He who is the Truth inspire every reader to be filled with the Spirit of Truth—the Holy Ghost.

Barry A. King

Since lying is a soul-damning sin, it is essential that we study this subject from every angle, lest we be cut off at the final judgment. I know of no other book that so thoroughly covers this subject—*The Sin of Lying*. It will certainly make the best of God's people stop and think! I recommend it to every Christian who is seeking to make his calling and election sure.

T. W. Barnes

The sound teaching and wholesome instruction given through the years by the author of this book, who is my father in the gospel, has greatly influenced my personal life and ministry for over thirty-six years. This exhaustive, scriptural, and thought-provoking message will, no doubt, serve to stir honest souls to examine themselves more thoroughly by the Word of God.

Danita Barnum Davis

The story is told of a saint dreaming he beheld the scourging of Jesus. As his ugly, metal-tipped cat-of-nine-tails slashed like sharp knives the bare back of our suffering Savior, the cruel and merciless soldier seemed to find fiendish glee in his sadistic work. In revulsion the dreamer cried out, whereupon the man turned, and for the first time the saint beheld his face. In horror he discovered the man was . . . himself! Reading *The Sin of*

Lying was a bit like this man's experience to me, for just when I felt assured I was free from guilt, I would turn a page and suddenly come face to face with a man resembling me. This book will be a most revealing and blessed help to all who are determined to be in the church without spot or wrinkle or any such thing.

David F. Gray

CHAPTER ONE

Introduction

The sin of lying is one of the most damnable and common sins of the human race. More people have been guilty of lying, in some form or other, than of any other sin which man has ever committed; and there is no doubt as to the final consequences of this sin if it is not repented of before one dies. The Bible plainly informs us, "All liars, shall have their part in the lake which burneth with fire and brimstone" (Revelation 21:8). On the other hand, we are informed by the psalmist David that only those who speak the truth from their heart will be allowed to dwell in God's holy hill and tabernacle (Psalm 15:1-2). A lying tongue is something which God hates, and any sane person could not conceive of God permitting anyone to enter heaven with something his Lord held such an attitude toward. The Lord further proved His attitude toward lying by slaying the first two people who were guilty of the sin of lying in the New Testament church, namely, Ananias and his wife, Sapphira. If God will not allow people who lie to remain in His church on this earth, He certainly is not going to permit them to enter heaven to defile it with their lying.

The sin of lying dates back to the Garden of Eden. Old Satan told his first lie to mankind when he lied to Eve. Therefore, he won the contemptible title of being "the father of lies" (John 8:44). All liars are going to spend eternity with their father in the lake of fire. I fear some people are not going to be so fond of their father, the devil, after they see what he has led them into.

Because the devil introduced this sin at the very time man fell from his high and holy state, it has become a part of his carnal nature to lie. David informed us, "The wicked are estranged from the womb: they go astray as soon as they be born, speaking lies" (Psalm 58:3). This goes to prove it is the fallen nature of man to lie. Many children are guilty of lying before they ever reach the age of accountability—before they know right from wrong.

Some of the most distinguished characters of the Bible have at some time or another been guilty of lying. Among this list we find Sarah (Abraham's wife), Isaac, Jacob, and David. No wonder David came to the place where he took so many precautions against committing this sin. (See Psalm 17:3; 141:3.) Many "men of high degree are a lie," as David said (Psalm 62:9). We run into so much lying at times until we think or say about the same thing as the psalmist: "I said in my haste, All men are liars." Thank God, it has always been true that there are a few people who tell the truth.

Hell is going to be filled with liars. If God would excuse the human race of all other damnable sins and send only those to hell who had some time or another told or acted a lie, hell would still be a densely populated place. Some people will go to hell for lying, if they are not careful, who would not [normally] tell a lie. The devil slips this sin over on many people unaware. You will be thoroughly convinced of the truth of this statement after you have finished reading the various forms of lying that we present further on in this book. . . . Remember, the Bible says all liars will spend an endless eternity in the burning pit—that is, those who do not repent of telling them.

Lying Defined

Lying is defined by Webster as being "an untruth, falsehood; something that creates a false impression," etc. A falsehood is defined as being a statement that distorts or suppresses the truth, and an untruth is defined as being an incorrect statement. Remember this, there is but one way around telling the truth, and that is to lie. Any time a person undertakes to avoid telling the truth, he is going to lie if he says or does anything otherwise. Remember this also, there is no rubber in the truth—you cannot stretch the truth—and there are no "truthful liars." Another good definition of a lie is given by a certain writer. He says, "A lie is universally defined as saying

17

to another that which is not true." God, help me and help you to tell the truth. One may think that he will gain by lying, and it may appear that way at first; but he will certainly find out to his own sorrow that it would have paid him to have told the truth, regardless of the first cost. We shall now proceed to our study of the various forms of lying.

CHAPTER TWO

Various Forms of Lying

1. Flattery

We are informed by the Word of God that the Lord is going to cut off all flattering lips (Psalm 12:3). All insincere praise and compliments come under this classification of lying. It is one of those forms of two-faced lying, for "with flattering lips and with a double tongue do they speak." Yes, flattering liars will pretend to your face that they think you have performed wonderfully, and then make fun or mock as soon as you turn your back or when they make mention of your efforts to others. One has to watch what he says when he compliments one for his singing, testifying, giving, preaching, musical performance, appearance, manner of dress, etc., or he will lie. He must tell them exactly what he thinks and feels from his heart, if he says anything and tells the truth.

We are living in an age of flattery. Almost everyone seems to be contaminated more or less with the spirit of flattering folk—lying to them. One cannot be a Christian or a true disciple of Jesus Christ and lie about anything. While the devil is the father of all lying, Jesus is the father of truth (John 14:6). Solomon was right when he said, "A flattering mouth worketh ruin" [Proverbs 26:28]. One of Israel's gross sins, which they committed while wandering in the wilderness, was their flattering God with their mouth (Psalm 78:36). Of all flattering and lying that one could be guilty of, there is none worse than flattering God. So be careful how you flatter any of God's people today, for God considers anything you do to them as though you did it to Him (Matthew 25:40). People who sin by flattering someone with a lying tongue are considered by the Lord to be very wicked (Psalm 5:9). Therefore, "let not your lips speak that which is not in your heart" (the Talmud).

2. Perverse Lying

While this is one of the various forms of lying, it is also another form of two-faced lying. It consists of lying by statements and reports by the same person which do not agree. One cannot tell the same thing differently and tell the truth. This form of lying is very destructive to the offender—"perverseness of transgressors shall destroy them" (Solomon) [Proverbs 11:3]. The wise man also advised us to put perverse lips far from us (Proverbs

4:24) and instructed us, "He that is perverse in his ways shall fall at once" [Proverbs 28:18]. Too, this is another form of disguised lying which one has to take much precaution against or he will find himself guilty of committing the sin.

3. Exaggeration

To exaggerate means to overstate, stretch, magnify, color, etc. So one has to watch and see that he does not exaggerate when he is sending in or giving reports of meetings, Bible conferences, camp meetings, conventions, healings, revivals, experiences, fishing or hunting trips, what he bought with a dollar, etc. Any time he overstates things, he is guilty of exaggeration—lying. Keep this in mind, there is no rubber in the truth—it cannot be stretched. The wise man said, "Add thou not unto his words, lest he reprove thee, and thou be found a liar" (Proverbs 30:6). So any kind of adding to the truth makes a lie out of it. It is a very easy matter to lie in this manner.

4. Diminishing

This form of lying is just opposite or reverse to the one just defined. It is committed by taking from instead of adding to. One is tempted to do this more often when he is reporting what others have done, especially if there is any ill will or jealousy buried in his unchristian heart. One is warned of the danger of this act in Revelation

22:19. What is true concerning God's Word is also true concerning taking away from or diminishing the truth.

5. Polite or Mannerly Lying

It takes great self-control and great sensitivity to the checks of the Spirit to order our conversations aright and steer clear of lying when it comes to everyday manners, customs, and living up to the modern rules of etiquette. David said, "They speak vanity every one with his neighbors . . . and with a double heart do they speak" [Psalm 12:2]. So when a person speaks with a double heart, he is not speaking out of a truthful heart. If there is any truth at all in his heart, it is contaminated with lies. One cannot tell the hostess that he has enjoyed a dinner when he has discovered flies in the beans, worms in the peas, or a hair in the butter, without telling a lie. Many have forgotten that God's Word says, "All liars shall have their part in the lake." These polite and mannerly lies will land one just as deeply in hell as any other lie that was ever told. It is almost impossible for one to live up to the rules of etiquette and the manners and customs of our day, in every respect, and tell the truth. Remember this, the old devil is a very polite fellow in many respects, and he is likely the instigator of some of the rules of etiquette that are laid down for us to follow, though they have been written by the hand of man. [Editor's note: One option is to find something positive about which to comment truthfully, while not discussing a negative aspect.]

6. Confidential Lying

"He that is of a faithful [truthful] spirit concealeth the matter" [Proverbs 11:13], but he that has an unfaithful (untruthful) spirit reports things and tells things that he has promised not to divulge. This divulging of confided news, secrets, information or whatever it might be is nothing less than confidential lying. When one divulges or makes known what he has promised not to tell, he has lied. Are you in the habit of telling things you promise not to tell? If so, repent and forsake such actions according to Proverbs 28:13 and Isaiah 55:7. The news that should be kept should not be such welcome news for a Christian, or for one who wants to shun the very appearance of evil and gain heaven for his eternal home. One should be as much afraid of this confided news and information, which is to never be told to anyone, as he would be of handling a rattlesnake or of meeting a lion in the wild forest without a weapon to defend himself. My friend, close your ears to this nature of gossip, and play safety first against confidential lying.

7. Tattling

Most tattlers tell lies one way or the other. They either add to, take from, or pretend to be a friend to both parties or all concerned. One cannot do thus and avoid lying. Solomon said, "A talebearer revealeth secrets" [Proverbs 11:13], and when he has done this, he has lied. Some tattlers can be classed as two-faced liars, while others may tell the truth regardless of what may take place. They often pretend to be a friend to the party to whom they divulge things, when they are an avowed enemy. Paul informed us that tattlers speak things which they ought not (I Timothy 5:13), and no one should tell lies. Many tattlers are going to hell for telling lies.

8. Cunning Lying

Cunning liars stay close to the truth to the extent that one often does not suspect them to be guilty of lying. Half-truths, three-quarter truths, nine-tenth truths, etc., when judged as a whole, are all lies. A little lying spoils any amount of truth and turns the whole thing into a lie, for no amount of truth will convert a lie into the truth. However, one may obtain forgiveness for telling lies by telling the truth and admitting he lied. One may get by man and his lie-detector machine with his lying, but he will never slip by the Lord. The Lord has a lie detector that is perfect and shows up everything that is not the truth. He let Peter use it once on some sly church folk, and it worked. We shall tell you more about God's lie detector further on in this book.

9. Promissory Lying

This may be a new form of lying to you from a title standpoint, but everyone who does not keep or fulfill his promises, or does not carry out what he has pledged himself to do, lies in this form. This form of lying is so serious and damnable that Solomon said, "Better is it that thou shouldest not vow, than that thou shouldest vow and not pay" [Ecclesiastes 5:5]. Many men and women have broken their promises to wed without any justifiable excuse or without a word of explanation or information and married another—lied. These promises one makes to God when sick, when out of work, when perplexed concerning what step or move to take or make, had better be kept; also those promises made to wife, husband, children, parents, neighbors, the grocer, to pastors by evangelists and to the evangelist by the pastor, to a church by a pastor and to the pastor by the church, to those who request our prayers, to the lender or to the borrower, etc. Much lying has been done along these lines.

When we begin to look into the sin of lying, one is made to question: "Lord, and who will be saved?" There is no need of pondering over this. He has already told us that none but those who speak the truth out of their hearts. (See Psalm 15:1-2.) This kind of lying has broken many hearts and destroyed much confidence. Let those who are thus guilty of lying repent, tell the truth, and regain the confidence lost by their lying.

Sorry to say, but there has been a bit of lying in this form or manner by (supposed-to-be) ministers of the gospel. Some or much of it may have been unintentional. Will that entirely clear them? Evangelists have lied by promising pastors and churches a campaign at a certain date or place, and the campaign was never conducted or agreeably postponed. On the other hand, pastors and churches have promised certain evangelists a meeting at some certain time or in the undesignated future, and the meeting has never materialized. Similar occurrences have existed between various ministers and churches concerning the pastorate. Some church boards have promised to consider calling a certain minister as pastor for their church and ignored their promise—lied. Then some preachers have promised certain churches that they would consider accepting their pastorate, which they never did. Brethren, these things should never occur among our churches and ministers. Our word should be our bond.

10. Santa Claus and Rabbit Egg Lying

Santa Claus lying is undoubtedly the most common form of lying that man is guilty of. More people have lied in this manner than in any other known form. The devil never hatched or introduced a bigger and more destructive lie than this one. It has robbed more children, and many of them with so-called Christian parents, of their belief in the story of Jesus than anything else that has ever confronted them. This form of lying often makes atheists out of children whose parents are professed Christians or have embraced the Christian faith. "Oh, wait," someone says, "one never lies in this manner!" Why not? Any untruth is defined as being a lie. There never has been a Santa Claus, as he is pictured to the children, and there never will be. There is no truth in such lying. No Christian should ever be, and had better not be, guilty of lying in this manner.

The devil has Santa Claus lying so timed that it is

told to the children right along with the story of Jesus, when Christians are celebrating the anniversary of their Savior's birth into the world, and at a time when the child's mind is tender and easily impressed. Then he has it timed for him to find out the falsehood of the story concerning Santa Claus just when he should be believing the true story of Jesus and just when he should be embracing the Christian faith for himself—just as he reaches the age of accountability. We are often made to wonder why many children turn their backs on the churches in which they were reared and have no confidence in God or the religion of their parents. If we could only trace such to the root cause, we would often find that the lying story about Santa Claus had destroyed their faith in Jesus, the Bible, and their parents' religion.

Rabbit egg lying is what might be called another one of those religious lies, and is timed similar to Santa Claus lying in that it is told at the very time we are celebrating the resurrection of Jesus Christ, which is the Christian's basic hope. (See I Corinthians 15:12-22; I Thessalonians 4:13-18; Job 19:25-27; Psalm 49:15; Isaiah 26:19.) There is positively no such thing as a rabbit laying eggs. People can cause their children to disbelieve the account of the resurrection of Jesus Christ by telling them such lies. May God help all those who are guilty of telling such lies to repent of the same and quit all kinds of lying, for the eternal good of themselves and their children. [Editor's note: One option is to identify such stories as imaginary.]

11. Pentecostal Lying

Probably you have never heard of this form of lying either. We call it Pentecostal lying because no one except Pentecostal people ever lie in this manner. Brother, the world has one on us here when we lie in this manner. Here is how it happens. We are about the only church today in which brothers [hug or] kiss the brothers and sisters [hug or] kiss the sisters with the "holy kiss" (Paul, II Corinthians 13:12) or the "kiss of charity" (love), as Peter called it (I Peter 5:14). Therefore, this form of lying is peculiar to Pentecostal people. Any time a brother kisses a brother or a sister a sister whom he or she does not love, they have lied by their actions. [See Luke 22:47.) This wholesale kissing of folk in the church will not do unless you love them all with a godly love. We do not mean by this that the kissing of the opposite sex is ever permissible in any of our churches. While this is in reality a true token of our Christian love for one another, it is nothing more than a good trap for hypocrites. It catches all the hypocrites, and the devil does not have to go to the trouble of running them down to catch them. The devil caught poor Judas Iscariot with this lie-trap, and he has caught many with it since then.

12. Lying Mottoes

While some Christians and people would not outright tell or act a lie, they will put up mottoes to lie for them. When a man hangs up a motto in his home that says,

"Christ is the head of this house," when his wife is the boss, such a motto lies for him to everyone who reads it. Any other motto that does not speak the truth as it actually is, lies. Pull down those lying mottoes and replace them with some that tell the truth, if you want to go to heaven!

13. Hypocritical Lying

Do hypocrites lie? One cannot be a hypocrite without lying (I Timothy 4:2). All professed Christians lie in this form. One has to be a real Christian, a possessor of the Spirit of Christ, to always tell the truth. Hypocrisy is defined as the act of pretending to be what one is not— lying actions. When a hypocrite shouts, dances, tries to act or appear happy, pretends to be burdened for lost souls and the work of the Lord in general (Philippians 3:18-19), falls on the floor when others are falling under the power of God, he is lying; for none of these things are real with him as long as he continues to be a hypocrite. Knowing that all hypocrites lie (I Timothy 4:2), how is it that one would ever aspire or even allow himself to be one? No wonder Isaiah said, "Fearfulness hath surprised the hypocrites. Who among us shall dwell with the devouring fire? . . . [and] everlasting burnings?" (Isaiah 33:14). The One whom John saw on the throne in heaven answered these two questions asked by Isaiah. He told John, "All liars, shall have their part in the lake which burneth with fire and brimstone" (Revelation 21:8). So it is a positive fact that all hypocrites are going to hell to burn forever, except they repent and live for God.

When Paul said, "Let love be without dissimulation" [Romans 12:9], he meant for us to be honest concerning the extent of and the manifestation of our love for our fellowman, the lost, the afflicted, and our brother in the Lord. The margin of many Bibles renders the word "dissimulation" to mean "hypocrisy." May God give us more of that Holy Ghost love (Romans 5:5) which flows of its own accord, without the aid of any human efforts, and we then can keep dissimulation (hypocrisy) out of all our gestures and acts of love toward our brother and fellowman. Brother or friend, God has His church and religion (salvation) fake proof. Any time one is not truthful and honest in his sayings and actions, he lies and thereby dooms himself. Hypocritical lying will certainly land one in hell (Revelation 21:8).

14. The Lying Smile

This form of lying might puzzle some of you if you were left to define it, but remember that this kind of lying would not be hard for a hypocrite to perform. (See I Timothy 4:2.) When our enemies meet us with a smile, they meet us with a lie. Many who appear to be "smiling joy" are often ready to burst into tears, and would if they would only let their inward feelings truly express themselves. There was no guile (deceit) about Jesus (I Peter 2:22), and there must be none found in His true followers. If Jesus ever smiled, there was no hypocrisy behind it. We conclude here by cautioning everyone not to judge anyone but himself concerning this form of lying, or any others.

15. Two-faced Lying

There seem to be many forms of this lying. Some of them we have already referred to. Any time one acts friendly toward another when he is his avowed enemy, he is guilty of this form of lying. Joab pulled this one on two good, honest men and men of great military worth to Israel, Abner and Amasa. (See II Samuel 3:26-28; 20:8-10.) This form of two-faced lying is generally prompted by some bad and wicked motives. Hitler and his generals pulled this form of two-faced lying on the Russians, to their own sorrow and annihilation as a ruling party or power.

Woe be unto those who lie in this form. Their day is coming. Joab had to be slain for this act before David and his successors could clear their hands before God of Abner's blood—due, I suppose, to the king's responsibility to God for all the acts of the nation. Backbiters, tattlers, gossipers, whisperers, and most of all, troublemakers in the church lie in this manner, more or less (Psalm 12:2). David said, "They delight in lies [of this nature]: they bless with their mouth [as Joab did to Amasa in II Samuel 20:9-10], but they curse inwardly [are boiling over with anger]" (Psalm 62:4).

16. Lying Impressions

To deliberately plan to leave a wrong impression by act or gesture is equally as bad as speaking a lie. Nor shall we act a lie by refusing to tell the whole truth. Playing the insanity role also comes under this heading. David played the insanity role before Achish, king of Gath, and his servants. "And David laid up these words in his heart, and was sore afraid of Achish the king of Gath. And he changed his behaviour before them, and feigned himself mad [crazy] in their hands, and scrabbled on the doors of the gate, and let his spittle fall down upon his beard" [I Samuel 21:12-13]. Though David managed to fool the king and make his escape by those lying impressions, he did not escape the guilt of lying. The Gibeonites fooled Joshua and the elders of Israel with their old worn-out clothes, sandals, stale bread, etc., to later become their servants for their lying impressions. (See Joshua 9:3-16.) God is keeping tab on all liars and will never take one of them into heaven unless he has been cleansed from such by the blood of Jesus Christ.

17. Silent Lying

Paul informed us that there are those "who hold the truth in unrighteousness" (Romans 1:18). One could do this by refusing to "amen" the preaching of the truth (Romans 1:25) or by refusing to speak or preach the truth himself. As the old saying goes, "Silence gives consent," or admits a thing is true if not contradicted by some word or action. There are times when a Christian is compelled to speak, or lie by keeping silent. Be a man, by God's grace, and stand up or speak in behalf of the truth when necessary. (See Psalm 94:16.)

18. "Amen," "Praise the Lord," and "Glory to God" Lying

Are you one of those who never heard of one lying in this manner? Any time a preacher informs his congregation: "Everybody who is happy say, 'Praise the Lord,' 'Glory to God,' or 'Amen,'" and they do so when they are not really happy, they lie in this manner or form. To make such declarations at any time in an insincere attitude is lying, for one has to speak the truth from his heart to avoid lying by such expressions, or any other kindred sayings (Psalm 15:2).

19. Lying Assertions

When the following statements are not true, they become lying assertions: "I am so happy," "I believe every promise in the Book" (Bible), "I fully trust God for both soul and body," "I enjoyed the sermon," "I enjoyed your singing," "I am so glad to see you," "I am glad you came," "Hurry back," "A grand time," "You are the idol of my heart," "You are the grandest person in the world," etc. Remember, all liars are going to be punished (Revelation 21:8).

20. Justificatory Lying

Remember this, most excuses are framed with lies. It is a dangerous thing to attempt to make an excuse. The blueprint for excuses calls for a certain amount of lying, and many people are making excuses all the time for their shortcomings as a Christian, neighbor, lender, borrower, foreman, employee or employer, etc. Excuses for this and excuses for that—lying instead of confessing their guilt. The best way around "justificatory lying" is to confess—shell down the truth (Proverbs 28:13). For "he who denies his guilt doubles his guilt" (the Talmud). In other words, he adds sin to sin, as a general rule, when he makes excuses. People who continually offer excuses for their shortcomings seldom mend, improve, or change their way of doing. On the other hand, people who confess generally change their way of living and acting. According to Jeremiah 3:11, a person who justifies himself is in a backsliding condition if not already backslidden. Job had this to say: "If I justify myself [which can only be done by making excuses], mine own mouth shall condemn me: if I say, I am perfect, it shall also prove me perverse" (Job 9:20). Justificatory liars are going where all other liars go—to the burning lake (Revelation 21:8).

21. Backtrack Lying

The title used for this form of lying is . . . colloquial. The true meaning of this form of lying is to retract, which means to take back something that has been said, to recall an utterance, to draw back or draw in, renounce, repudiate, etc. One has to watch about taking back what he has said or promised to do, especially if it is done in the attitude of disregarding those concerned, or due to the lack of interest in fulfilling his promises, else he will be found a liar in the sight of God. This is a form of lying that is hard to distinguish or discover without the aid of the Holy Spirit, either in our own life and actions or in the lives of others. Much precaution should be taken when it comes to judging the guilt of others concerning this form of lying, for without the aid of the Holy Spirit, man is limited in his judgment to the seeing of the eye and hearing of the ear—which often leads to an erroneous conclusion or opinion. (See Matthew 7:1-5.)

22. Lying by Denial

This form of lying is committed by one denying what he has formerly said or done and is often committed by one denying his guilt when guilty. Anyone can readily see that such an act as this is nothing but lying. However, some people become very bold in their lying in this manner. Sarah, Abraham's wife, laughed concerning the Lord promising her and Abraham a son when they were both old and stricken with age, and when she discovered that her laughter had displeased the Lord she denied committing the act to His face and in contradiction to His own knowledge and observation of her act when she knew she was guilty. According to the Scripture, she let a spirit of fear frighten her into lying by denying her guilt (Genesis 18:1, 9-15). This, however, did not justify her for lying to the Lord; neither did it take away her guilt. She had lied, and the Lord had to rebuke her to her face for her sin. May we not expect God to deal severely with us if we, too, lie in this manner? I think so, for God is no respecter of persons. He deals with all alike (Acts 10:34).

Deny what you say and do and go to hell if you prefer, is the stand that God takes regardless of who you are. An honest confession for this sin of lying will keep one from going to the devil's eternal abode (Proverbs 28:13; I John 1:9). Keep in mind, "He who denies his guilt doubles his guilt," according to the Talmud.

The person who says he has forgotten certain things when he does remember, lies in this manner. Many are those who have lied by denying their guilt or by claiming to have forgotten things they faintly or definitely remember. Hell is staring such liars right in the face, the same as all other liars (Revelation 21:8).

23. Deceptive Lying

In a sense, all lying may be deceptive; but any time one undertakes to deceive another, he will very likely lie in this manner. Solomon said, "A deceitful witness speaketh lies" [Proverbs 14:25]. All kinds of divinations, witchery, fortunetelling, false claims of being led of God in order to deceive people, false interpretations of the Scriptures, false interpretation of tongues, false reports concerning organizations, bank assets, investments, stocks, bonds, etc., all lead to and constitute this form of lying. One had better be led of God or know he is telling the truth when he publicly declares such to be true.

This kind of lying not only has its bad effect upon the guilty party, but it dooms so many of the hearers or receivers. Look at what happened to the "man of God" to whom the false prophet lied, as recorded in I Kings 13.

The man of God lost his life as a result of being deceived by the false prophet's lies. Many honest-hearted people will likewise lose their souls for believing some lying preacher's instructions concerning his theory of the plan of salvation. There is but one way to be saved (Ephesians 4:4-6), and that is according to what is laid down in the New Testament by Jesus and His apostles. (See John 3:3-5; Acts 2:37-39; 4:10-12; Mark 16:15-16; II Thessalonians 1:7-10.)

24. Psychological Lying

Psychological lying is psychology falsely applied, if I understand correctly the basic principles of psychology. (See I Timothy 6:20.) When one pretends to be interested in something when he is not, or vice versa, in order to deceive another person into doing or not doing something, he has lied in this form. It goes like this: a certain man's wife was in the habit of visiting her relatives when she decided to do so, regardless of whether it pleased him or not. He first tried to hinder her by outright objecting and possibly refusing to let her have money for her fare and the expenses of the trips. Such tactics failed. He then decided that he would deceive her into staying by the use of a little lying psychology. The next time she spoke of going home, he pretended to be highly in favor of her going and offered to assist in almost every way imaginable. She decided he must have another woman or something unusual in mind that demanded her absence, so she persistently stayed at home, as she figured, to his sorrow and to her good pleasure. This was the whole aim of all of his plans and actions—to get her to stay at home—but the poor fellow lied to accomplish his desires. God's Word does not make any allowances for any form of lying. (See Revelation 21:8.)

Preachers, you cannot pretend to be indifferent about a pastorate, a meeting, or an official position in some organization when you are much concerned, if you do so to carry out your aims or gain your desires. This will apply to many things in or out of the church. Many high-powered salesmen employ this method of lying to sell their merchandise. They are selling their souls to the flames of hell while they sell their merchandise. God, give us more understanding of all forms of lying and grace to always tell the truth. You wives had better not employ this method to keep your husbands at home. Make it a matter of prayer and God will keep him at home, by some means of His own choosing.

25. Courtship Lying

Samson set the example of this form of lying. He lied to his girlfriend with little apprehension of the consequences to follow. He was soon robbed of his God-given strength, his liberty or freedom, his eyesight, and his girlfriend, and he died with the uncircumcised (unsaved). (See Judges 16:10-31.) This pretending to love a boyfriend or girlfriend has led to many a broken heart, and in some cases an act of suicide or an unhappy marriage. Love from only one party after marriage does not make for a happy union or home. This form of lying often leads to divorce, a remarriage on the part of one or both, and then adultery and hell. It is going to be a bad thing for one who enters hell to be able to trace his or her steps back to courtship lying, either on his part or the part of his companion. Boys and girls, men and women, widows and widowers, you can certainly gain nothing by lying during courtship. Do not pretend to love another when you have no love in your heart for them. A Christian will rob himself of all his spiritual power and blessing if he lies in this manner and also will have his name blotted out of "God's family record book," the Book of Life. (See Exodus 32:33; Psalm 69:27-28.)

26. Matrimonial Lying

The marriage vow is seldom taken very seriously anymore. Men and women are thus lying to ministers, judges, those who officiate, and God when they do not carry out the promises made at this time. These promises are made before God and man and are never to be broken except by death. This form of lying leads to separations, divorces, remarriages, wrecked homes, scattered families who become strangers to each other, fatherless, motherless and homeless children, adultery, fornication, heartaches, misery, and hell (Revelation 21:8).

The home life of America and the whole world is headed for the rocks, and this form of lying is playing its part in accomplishing these things. If man does not repent of his lying and the many other sins he is committing, God will have to bring him into judgment and punish him for his ungodly ways. Of all people who should tell the truth concerning holy matrimony, it is those who profess to be Christians, and it pays anyone and everyone else to tell the truth.

27. Comradeship Lying

Paul cautioned Christians, "Lie not one to another" (Colossians 3:9). This form of lying is often carried on between husband and wife, partners in business, and various associates. This breaks up homes, dissolves partnerships, causes friends to become enemies, etc. Remember, one's lack of being a Christian does not give him permission to lie. Anyone who lies is going to reap his sin. (See Galatians 6:7; Numbers 32:23.)

28. Undermining Lying

This is a form of lying which is carried on to injure a person by cheating him out of a position such as a church or an office in the church; to keep an evangelist from being given a meeting; to accomplish the removal of some official in the church or a business concern; to destroy someone's reputation or prestige, etc. Much lying is done in this manner in all walks of life, and many people will go to hell for it. The writer lost two jobs or positions with oil companies before he entered the ministry due to this kind of lying. However, the Lord blessed him with better employment each time. To you who may be lied on in this manner in the future, keep in mind that "all things work together for good to them that love God" (Romans 8:28). Keep sweet in your soul and stay humble; God will work things out for you and sooner or later punish the liar. "For he that will love life, and see good days, let him refrain his tongue from evil [undermining lying], and his lips that they speak no guile" (I Peter 3:10). One never gains anything worthwhile or of any lasting good by lying.

29. Official Lying

We may look for "wickedness in high places" these days. David said, "Surely . . . men of high degree are a lie" [Psalm 62:9]. In Revelation 2:2 we read: "Thou hast tried them which say they are apostles, and are not, and hast found them [to be] liars." We do not like to think of men of such rank and file ever being guilty of lying, but it is sometimes the case, to our sorrow and their shame. Then on the other hand, we thank God that some of our leading men of both the church and governmental affairs still tell the truth. Those who would refrain from lying for personal gain or purposes should refuse to lie for corporations, insurance companies, railroads, banks, governments, churches, or what not (Revelation 21:8). Official reports concerning these various firms and associations should contain nothing but the truth. Remember, if we lie for the other fellow, we become a partaker of his sins, which the Scriptures warn us against (I Timothy 5:22).

41

30. The Lie of Mooching

This form of lying does not necessarily include the hobo or professional tramp, just the person who claims to have had a streak of bad luck, some serious illness, or misfortune of life. There is so much of this form of lying until one never knows who to help or who is really in need of food, clothing, or a few nights' lodging. The person often wants money to buy liquor, dope, tobacco, or to gamble with instead of something to purchase food and other necessities. These mooching liars will come right into the church telling their lies. They seem to take pleasure in infringing upon the charity of religious institutions and their constituents. Poor fellows, they come to a place seeking death where they should be seeking life, and do not realize what they are doing.

31. Pitiful or Hobo Lying

Many professional tramps or hobos tell little truth when they ask for something to eat. They often pretend to be hungry to get something to carry with them to eat later. They could get it just the same by telling the truth. The writer knows of one professional beggar who claimed to be dumb as well as partly paralyzed, but who forgot and began to talk during a conversation. That lie I caught him in made me disbelieve the rest of his story, and consequently I did not help him anymore. It never pays to lie, here or hereafter. (See Galatians 6:7-8; Revelation 21:8.)

Preachers need to be careful about relating too much

concerning their needs or conditions financially. Even when such stories contain nothing but the truth, people are often made to question the veracity of them. "Shun the very appearance of evil" is good advice to always bear in mind and observe.

32. Professional and Qualification Lying

People who claim to be trained or experienced in any line of work for which they are not, lie when they make such claims. Employers have been imposed upon so much by this mode of lying until they have taken many precautions against employing such men, and yet some of them get by all their examinations and requirements. Men claim to be carpenters, mechanics, painters, machinists, pipe fitters, welders, various kinds of oil field workers, etc., who never worked a day at such trades. Any kind of a false claim is a lie.

Two boys I once knew hired out as a dishwasher and cook. The proprietor assigned their work for the preparation of the noon lunch, instructing the one who had posed as a cook to cook a certain large pan full of rice. She then took off to town to return and find almost everything in the kitchen full of cooked rice and the boys gone—nothing but rice for her boarders to eat for lunch. To her sorrow, shame, and disappointment her lying cook and dishwasher could not be located.

33. Mechanic Lying

This form of lying is so common today until one

almost expects to get swindled when he carries his car to a garage for repairs. Many mechanics lie concerning what is out of operating order about the car, or lie concerning the repairs made and the standard price for the same. People are often charged for repairs that are never made and for parts that are never installed. The writer heard of a garage owner who gave a shop foreman a "once over" for not using his pencil more when charging for parts and repairs. What is true concerning the car mechanic is often true with other mechanics—they lie, too, concerning the things they repair. The writer knows of two shop foremen in authorized Chevrolet garages who are known for their honesty and veracity. As a rule they have more work than they can turn out. Their employers gain by their truthfulness and honesty. Too bad, but many will go to hell for this form of lying (Revelation 21:8).

34. Parental Lying

Parents often lie to their children . . . concerning many different things, which is a very bad thing to do. One who lies habitually to his children need not expect anything less of them (Galatians 6:7). Children often blame their parents for their lying when they know their parents have lied to them—set the example before them. Some children detect or discover so much lying in their parents, until they must say about the same thing that we find recorded in Jeremiah 16:19—"Surely our fathers have inherited lies."

Parents should not lie by telling their children, "Finish your work and we will go fishing or take an outing," "Be nice and mannerly and mother will give you a dime," "Just as sure as you do certain things, I will whip you," "If you don't do what I have assigned you, I will not let you go," etc., and never do what they tell and promise their children. God help all of us parents to be cautious and tell our children the truth. No wonder we have so many liars in the world today! Many parents are training their children to lie by lying to them or before them.

35. Jealous Lying

Jealous lying is that form of lying which is prompted by jealousy. It is said that "jealousy is as cruel as death" and that is true. Jealousy has prompted many people to lie even to the extent that it caused someone to lose his life or be seriously injured. Jealous children often lie on their brothers and sisters to their parents. Jealous deacons, musicians, singers, Sunday school teachers, etc., lie on one another to their own shame and to the reproach of the whole church and cause of Christ. Jealousy blinds people, spiritually speaking, and they never see the harm they will cause by lying before they do such a thing. People in almost all walks of life—the barber, doctor, dentist, grocer, druggist, mechanic, carpenter, brick mason, electrician, lawyer, welder, etc.—are at times overcome with a spirit of jealousy that prompts them to lie on their fellowman. But there are not any excuses, in the sight of the Lord, which justify one to lie.

36. Rationing Lying

This form of lying has taken in many people, including a host of professed Christians, and may damn many other folk when we are involved in war again. If people do not repent of this form of lying, God will have to enlarge hell to be able to put all of them in the lake of fire. It has been enlarged in the past (Isaiah 5:14); I am sure it can be done again. This lying about rent prices, cost of repairing apartments, and dwelling houses; lying to obtain gasoline, tires, tubes, cars, bicycles, sugar, and anything that is or was rationed, is just another way for one to lose his soul. Just think of the penalty imposed for this form of lying by Uncle Sam—"ten years imprisonment or $10,000.00 fine, or both." Uncle Sam is about as hard on liars as God is.

One does not have to lie to get what is due him of that which is rationed. He lies to get more than his allotted share, and that is a very unfair thing. It is far from living up to the Golden Rule—doing unto others as you would have them to do unto you. Many traps are set for those who lie these days, and they are catching a host of them. If we had definite statistics on all forms of lying, I am sure that this one would take in or include about as many as any other form except Santa Claus lying. The devil is taking advantage of almost everything that comes up these days to use it to induce people to lie. In ages to come, this may be referred to as a lying age—a time when almost everyone lied in some form or another. "If the righteous [those who do not lie] scarcely be saved [escape the devil's lying traps], where shall the ungodly [the lying church member] and the [lying] sinner appear?" [See I Peter 4:18.] The Bible answers this question: "The wicked [habitual liars and sinners] shall be turned into hell, and all the nations that forget God [and lie]." (See Psalm 9:17.)

It matters not at what time in the future you may read this book, you should know something of the time when the author wrote it—during World War II.

37. Income Tax Lying

Any time one signs his name to a declaration form for estimated income or to the original final return form used for computing his income and either of them contain, to his certain knowledge, false statements or figures, he has lied, even if someone else filled out the form or declaration for him. Uncle Sam is calling men and corporations into his courts every day to answer for this form of lying, and to pay the penalty when proved guilty. God is going to call the same gentlemen and ladies to come before His court, the Great White Throne Judgment, some of these days—about one thousand years after the righteous dead have been resurrected and gone on to their glorious rewards—to give account of this form of lying, and all other kinds too. He is not going to let any of them slip by or go unpunished. (See Revelation 21:8, 27.)

This is where money will cause one to lie and lose his soul if he is not careful—by lying to save his money or to keep from paying it out for taxes imposed by the federal government. Truly, "the love of money is [turns out to be] the root [cause] of all evil" (including lying). (See I Timothy 6:10; Acts 5:1-11.) It is so easy for one to let his heart get attached to money to where it controls him instead of his controlling what money he possesses. My friend and brother in the Lord, keep your money under your control if you intend to make it to heaven, and do not let it prompt you to lie under any circumstances, this income tax lying included.

38. Immigrational Lying

This is that kind of lying one does to obtain passage from one country to another when he feels that he does not have sufficient or justifiable reasons to obtain the passport or permission. Some people would lie their way into heaven if they could, but God has a total ban on all liars entering His country (Revelation 21:27).

The writer observed and inquired into some of the rules of immigration once when going into and returning from Canada—which rules are not so strict for Americans and Canadians. As I was returning to the States, a United States immigration officer ordered one man taken off the train before we crossed the line into Portal, North Dakota. I inquired of him why he had refused the man entrance, and he informed me that he had lied to him when cross-questioned, and he informed me that if a man was ever caught lying, they could deny him entrance on that point alone, regardless of how many justifiable reasons he had to offer. So lying alone will keep people from making the passage from this earth to

God's country (heaven) regardless of all the good deeds they have performed (Matthew 7:21-23; Revelation 21:27). It has kept many a poor soul from entering our wonderful country where much freedom is enjoyed. It looks as though people would learn that it never pays to lie and that no liar will be permitted to enter heaven.

39. Treacherous Lying

A treacherous liar is one who betrays people of his own state, church or country by lying. One who pretends to be true and loyal when he is just the opposite at heart is a treacherous liar. Such was Judas Iscariot. According to Zephaniah 3:4-7 there have been some prophets, priests, and preachers guilty of committing this form of lying. To betray one's confidence that he has placed in us by lying actions or statements is nothing less than treacherous lying. We read in Habakkuk 1:13, "Wherefore lookest thou upon them that deal treacherously, and holdest thy tongue when the wicked devoureth the man that is more righteous than he?" Such as this is often the case. A man or woman, who is living immorally and indulging in all kinds of wicked acts and sins, will often lie on the righteous man or sister in a very treacherous manner. Do not worry; God, in due time, will bring such people into judgment to account for their wicked acts and lying (Ecclesiastes 12:14).

40. Threatening Lying

When one makes threats that he does not intend to

carry out, he lies in this manner. This lying to scare folk or children into doing things is going to get some into trouble with God, if not others. This form of lying is commonly known and referred to as blackmail when such threats are sent to people, corporations, judges, prosecuting attorneys, etc. through the U.S. mail service. Parents cannot threaten to punish their children to get them to do or not do things unless they mean to do what they say; otherwise they lie in this manner. When the pastor of a church threatens to resign unless the church folk do certain things, he, too, had better be speaking the truth from his heart or he will lie in this manner and go to hell as the final consequence of such, unless he repents. Employers often make threats to their employees that they have no intention of carrying out, and quite often the employees do the same thing—they threaten to quit if certain things are not granted or carried out. One is forced to either carry out his threats, apologize, or lie. Church and organizational officials need to be careful or they will lie in this manner, almost before they are aware of what they are doing. David said, "I will take heed to my ways, that I sin not with my tongue," and he later prayed, "Set a watch, O Lord, before my mouth; keep the door of my lips." [See Psalm 39:1; 141:3.] How easy it is for one to sin by lying in this manner!

41. Relationship and Acquaintance Lying

Those who deny being related to those who are their blood kin, and those who deny knowing those with whom they are acquainted and associated in and out of the church, lie in this manner. Pride often prompts this form of lying. Paul must have suffered or experienced something of this nature and was making reference to it when he said, "As unknown, and yet well known" (II Corinthians 6:9). The apostle Peter lied in this manner the night Jesus was brought before Caiaphas, the high priest, to be tried. (See John 18:15-18, 24-27.)

One could lie in this manner concerning his spiritual relationship, and will, unless he is frank to admit it as Paul did. When Paul was being tried before Felix he acknowledged or confessed: "After the way which they call heresy, so worship I the God of my fathers" [Acts 24:14]. Paul was not ashamed of his religious affiliation (Romans 1:16); neither did he allow himself to lie in this manner as some church folk do.

42. Clinic and Hospital Lying

We do not mean by this title that all doctors and nurses are liars and that none of them ever tell the truth. The writer is personally acquainted with some doctors who have a reputation of being truthful. But like all other professions, there are some doctors and nurses who either figure it is best for them to lie or they have acquired the lying habit. This is likely the reason the psalmist informed God's children: "It is better to trust in the Lord [One who never lies and cannot lie] than to put confidence in man" [Psalm 118:8]. And if we all realized or believed that "whoso putteth his trust in the Lord shall be safe" (Proverbs 29:25), I am sure there would be more of God's children trusting Him for their healing, health, and protection from all contagious diseases instead of running the risk of being lied to and being given something or being operated on in a manner that would hasten them into eternity.

43. Business Lying

Some people think that they cannot carry on a business successfully without lying, at least occasionally. Paul admonished us, "Lie not one to another" (Colossians 3:9). One who lies to sell drives his customers away from his place of business, as a general rule, and sends them elsewhere to purchase what they want. A man does not have to tell many lies to gain a reputation for lying, for his lying will soon find him out, or be generally known. Some businessmen are so aware of the effect that lying produces upon their business until they will dismiss clerks and employees who lie. They even go so far as to instruct their employees to always tell the truth about what they are selling. One will seldom go broke for telling the truth.

44. Filthy Lucre Lying

This form of lying covers more than "business lying." People who do not operate any kind of a business establishment, lie for financial gain. The writer knows of a man who lied about the price of some chickens once to buy the chickens fifteen cents per head cheaper for his own use. He did not save more than two dollars by telling that lie, and thereby doomed and assured himself of going to a devil's hell—provided he never repented of the act. Solomon says, "The getting of treasures by a lying tongue is a vanity tossed to and fro of them that seek death" (Proverbs 21:6).

The apostle Paul informed us: "The love of money is the root of all evil." "The love of money" has caused many people to lie. In fact, there are only a few people who have not been induced to lie from this source. Without the Holy Ghost to guard the doors of our lips and minds, almost any of us might lie at one time or another for the gain of "filthy lucre."

45. The Lie of Sorcery and Fortunetelling

According to the Bible, all enchanters, magicians, sorcerers, fortunetellers, and spiritualist mediums are liars. "Therefore hearken not ye to your . . . diviners, nor to your dreamers, nor to your enchanters, nor to your sorcerers . . . for they prophesy a lie unto you" (Jeremiah 27:9-10). These fortunetellers are absolutely nothing but lie peddlers. Many of them go around with fortunes, which have been printed for years, to sell in rotation to those who are foolish enough to buy one of their lies. It is estimated that 80,000 or more of these wizards and magicians are making a living off the American people now, selling them lies. If they only collected $2,000 a year each, it would amount to $160,000,000 annually that Americans are paying for this form of lying.

Statistics show that the amount is much greater than the figures given. We must have a host of lie customers in America as well as a goodly number of liars. The sad part about this is: the devil is going to get the liars and their customers too. (See Revelation 21:8; I Timothy 5:22.) King Saul ate his last meal or lunch with the old witch of Endor. God's people had better heed His Word and have nothing to do with any of these consulters with familiar spirits, necromancers, wizards, diviners, fortunetellers, sorcerers, and magicians. (See Deuteronomy 18:9-14; Micah 5:12; Galatians 5:19-21; Nahum 3:4-6.)

46. Bribery Lying

This form of lying is committed by those who accept gifts and money to render false reports, false accounts, and make false statements as desired by the one who bribes them. We have a case of this nature recorded in Matthew 28:11-15, which reads as follows: "Now when they were going, behold, some of the watch came into the city, and shewed unto the chief priests all the things that were done. And when they were assembled with the elders, and had taken counsel, they gave large money unto the soldiers [who had stood guard at our Lord's grave], saying, Say ye, His disciples came by night, and stole him away while we slept. And if this come to the governor's ears, we will persuade him, and secure you. So they took the money, and did as they were taught"—lied about the whole affair.

Much of this kind of lying is purchased with gifts

today from those who want to earn money in an easy way—they think! The writer knows of a certain man who will lie for money in this manner even though it swindles poor people out of their possessions. In one instance, it is reported that he obtained the signature of an old couple, who had an interest in some real estate worth thousands of dollars, for the meager sum of seventy-five dollars. He lied to them and probably told them it would be the seventy-five dollars or nothing, so they took him at his word and signed the document or deed. He probably received several thousand dollars of bribery money for this lying transaction, and felt that he had put over a great deal and made a wonderful financial haul. But he will find out on that great reckoning day, when he stands before the Judge of the whole earth, that it is going to be a terrible deal to doom and damn his soul. Keep this in mind—it never pays to lie (Revelation 21:8).

According to Job 15:34, "The congregations of hypocrites shall be desolate, and fire shall consume the tabernacles of bribery." So those who bribe others to lie will suffer the tortures of the eternal fire the same as those whom they thus entice to lie. Be careful lest you be a partaker of other men's sins. (See I Timothy 5:22; Isaiah 33:14.)

47. Careless and Reckless Lying

To be a careless and reckless liar means that one is heedlessly paying no attention to the truthfulness or untruthfulness of his statements and does not consider what the consequences of such lying may be. David let a spell of this kind of lying come on him one time, when he was fleeing from Saul and stopped at Nob to get some bread and a sword from the priest, Ahimelech. He told him three lies in one statement or right in succession (I Samuel 21:2). The king had not sent him on a business errand, neither had he told him to keep his mission a secret from others, and David was journeying alone, though he pretended that a number of men were accompanying him.

A reckless and careless liar is more dangerous than a reckless driver of an automobile or a careless pilot of an airplane. David occasioned the death of eighty-five priests and all the inhabitants of Nob by his careless lying. Read I Samuel 21:1-10 with 22:7-22 and see for yourself that I am informing you correctly about this incident. The city of Nob has never been rebuilt. It passed into oblivion as a result of David's lying, and many people and cities have gone likewise since then for some person's reckless lying. It is bad enough for one to lie when it only affects himself. It is a terrible and very wicked act when it produces results as in the case just related. No wonder David had to pray for God to create a clean heart in him, set a watch before his mouth, and keep the doors of his lips (Psalm 51:10; 141:3). A person who lies to get himself out of some predicament generally gets into something worse. (See I Samuel 21:1-2, 10-13.) The best way out is to tell the truth and do some repenting too. (See Proverbs 28:13; I John 1:7, 9.) A person who allows himself to talk too freely will sooner or later be guilty of lying, and possibly in this manner. (See Proverbs 10:19; Ecclesiastes 5:1-2.)

If you ever took notice, you have seen that a wreck seldom, if ever, stops a reckless driver from driving recklessly. He may soon have another wreck. The same is true with this kind of liar. David went right on after lying to Ahimelech and played the insanity role before Achish, king of Gath, when he discovered they were thinking of finishing him off while they had him in their hands—just another spell of lying. As one writer has said, "One lie leads to another; we have to tell the second to hide the first." David, though a man after God's own heart, often found himself in the predicament of Romans 7:15-23. You and I should live in the experience of Romans 8:1-4; then and only then or thereafter would we be kept from lying or be empowered to always tell the truth.

48. Sectarian Lying

Much of this kind of lying goes on today. One church lies concerning the other, and this denomination lies on that one. All of this kind of lying is prompted by that sectarian spirit which possesses so many ministers and laymen of various denominations and organizations. This sectarian lying will send men and women to hell the same as all other lying (Revelation 21:8). As the old saying goes, "If we would keep things swept clean around our own doors, we would be kept busy at home most of the time," and would not be meddling with the other man's affairs so much.

49. Political and Diplomatic Lying

Do not run for an office or get into politics if you cannot take lying. Political and diplomatic scheming calls for much lying. Some church leaders and officials play politics when conducting a church election, and the devil gets most of them to lie before it is over. God gets out of church business and elections when His people start this diplomatic lying. Some say, "But you have to use a little diplomacy to put things over." Possibly so, if they are to be put over man's way, or as he desires things to go; but it is not needed when we go God's way and follow the leading of the Holy Ghost. Have we forgotten the promises of God along this line? Read Proverbs 3:5-6; Psalm 37:5, 23; Jeremiah 10:23; John 16:13; Romans 8:14; James 4:3 and see if God does not promise to lead us in all things pertaining to the work of the Lord. (See also Acts 1:19-23; 9:10-19; 13:1-4; 16:6-11.)

When church matters are carried out man's way, they are seldom what God would have, and we would do well to remember God's exhortation along this line as found in Isaiah 55:8-9: "For my thoughts are not your thoughts, neither are your ways my ways, saith the Lord. For as the heavens are higher than the earth, so are my ways higher than your ways, and my thoughts than your thoughts." The poor lost world is to be pitied and shown sympathy for the way they carry on things, but the way some of God's (supposed-to-be) leading children do business for Him is a reproach to His name and church. The very idea of lying to put things over for God! God had rather we just leave His business undone than to mess it up with a lot of lying. Business, such as general elections, local church elections, and any other nature, that is put over by lying, will never accomplish anything worthwhile. God is determined that His church shall be established by truth and nothing but the truth. All of us will do well to keep this in mind. We should all know that "we can do nothing against the truth" (II Corinthians 13:8). This political and diplomatic lying has about ruined some churches and organizations, if not all of them, and most all the nations and governments of this sin-cursed world. The devil has almost everyone ready to change climates (Revelation 21:8, 27).

50. Propaganda Lying

This kind of lying is done mostly in time of war, both among the nations and our various churches and organizations. When we go to war naturally or religiously, this propaganda lying always begins. The devil has someone on the job to start it and then hosts of dupes to pass it on to others.

There are several purposes for this propaganda lying; but, after all, the aims sought for never materialize, if you will take note or check after it, whether it is done by national patriots or church officials and lay members. Propaganda lying is done to stir up hatred against the opposing armies or churches and organizations—also to build morale and increase loyalty to the church or nation with which one is associated. It is also shifted to the enemy forces and territory by radio, by news leaflets dropped from the air, and by traitors to make them suspicious of one another and afraid to fight or oppose their national or religious enemy—also to divide and weaken them. Can God approve of all this ungodly work and devilish lying being carried on in His church? A thousand times no! We must either keep our tongues from speaking guile and deceit or get out of God's church—rather be put out (Exodus 32:33; Psalm 69:27-28). We cannot build anything for God that will stand if it is built upon a faulty foundation of hay, wood, stubble, lying, and deceit. So "let every man take heed how he buildeth thereupon" (I Corinthians 3:10). As the good old song goes, "Everything that is not of Jesus shall go down, shall go down"—yea, to the pits of hell or the bottomless pit (Revelation 21:8).

51. Strategical Lying

Strategical lying is that lying which is done concerning the supposed-to-be size, movement, location, casualty list, etc., of the Army, Navy, and Air Force. There has been much of this form of lying done during the present war [World War II], and possibly will continue as long as we have wars. If England had transferred as many troops, equipment and supplies to Singapore as she reported through the press and over the radio, before this base was taken by the Japanese, the Japanese never would have been able to take it. So most of her defense there proved to be nothing but lies, and she lost a valuable base and what men she had stationed there, too. After all, there was nothing gained by all that lying—she lost. We will do the same thing if we lie in this manner or any other way. We will lose here and then lose our soul in the end. Consider this too: men who lie for churches, nations, business firms, lodges, and labor unions are going to hell, though they were the middle man or just passed the lie. Remember, all men and Christians are warned by Paul not to "be partaker of other men's sins: keep thyself pure"—do not lie for anyone (I Timothy 5:22).

52. National and International Lying

This form of lying played its part in plunging the whole world into war this last time. As for lying, this form did play the major part and pride took the other. Pride of race and international lying are the two principal causes of this war, and the whole world knows it. These are facts which cannot be denied. There may have been many other minor causes, but no principal ones in comparison to these two.

There has been so much national and international lying done until peace treaties are not worth the paper they are written on. England, France, Czechoslovakia, Poland, and the whole world trusted that Hitler only wanted what he first asked for from the two last-named nations; but to their sorrow, and not very much to their surprise, they soon found out that he was lying. He gained so much apparently, to begin with, by his lying until it seems that he thought that he might take the whole world by the same method. Thank God, his lying did not win for him what he hoped to gain. He lost all he had to begin with and all he gained momentarily, by his lying, and brought his people to servitude and national disgrace. The whole world needs to learn by this example that it does not pay to lie. But this lesson is to be learned the hard way—by experience—and it is doubtful if any nations will take heed and only a very few individuals, to the extent that they will stop their lying.

The Antichrist is due to come into power by lying, not only in this manner but in every other manner or form conceivable, known or unknown. "And then shall that Wicked be revealed, . . . even him, whose coming is after the working of Satan with all power and signs and lying wonders" (II Thessalonians 2:8-9). The devil has begun to supply many nations with lying leaders and dictators. His next move will be to deceive and rule the whole world by a lying genius, the Antichrist. People generally fall for what they are accustomed to, and they are receiving ample training along this line. One faces liars and lying almost every way he turns today. The devil started out by deceiving man by lying, and he is going to finish the same way. I suppose that he has deceived and damned more souls in this manner than in all other ways and means combined. In fact, there is some form of lying employed by the devil and his subjects in everything they do and undertake. What else could we expect of a spirit or being, and of those influenced and controlled by him, in which there is no truth—nothing but lies and a lying spirit?

Those who expect and desire to keep out of hell and go to heaven when they die or leave this world, had better get Jesus to free them from all of Satan's clutches and fill them with His Spirit of truth, the Holy Ghost. (See John 14:16-17; 15:26; 16:7-13.)

53. Pulpit Lying

All ministers need to watch and see that everything they say over the sacred desk is truth. To say, "I will be through in just a minute," and then preach on for a half an hour is nothing but lying. . . . Do not say, "We will just read one more Scripture and then close," unless you mean to do that. Other similar statements run like this: "I will not hold you long," and preach two hours; "Stand and we will be dismissed," and keep the audience standing fifteen or twenty minutes before the benediction is pronounced. This is some more of that careless lying and will soon lead to reckless lying. Ministers who lie in this manner should obey Daniel's instructions to Nebuchadnezzar and "break off thy sins [lying] by righteousness [telling the truth]." How can we expect our congregations to be truthful if we practice lying before them and excuse ourselves for doing so? Remember, like priest like people. Some of the lay members' and lost sinners' lying is no worse than this, and we preach and teach that all liars are going to hell. If all means all, there are none who are going to escape—preachers, lay members or sinners who never knew God.

54. Camouflaged Lying

This form of lying might be employed and practiced in several ways. Quite often people lie to cover or hide (camouflage) their sins, shortcomings, evil dispositions, and evil intentions. Solomon said, "He that hideth [camouflages] hatred with lying lips . . . is a fool," and a big one at that; for such is sure to land one in hell (Revelation 21:8), if not repented of (Luke 13:5). In this sense lying is used as the camouflage materials, according to Isaiah 28:15, 17: "We have made lies our refuge, . . . and under falsehood have we hid ourselves . . . and the hail [of God's judgment] shall sweep away the refuge [camouflage] of lies, and the waters shall overflow the hiding place"— which they camouflaged with lies.

Quite often people endeavor to camouflage their lying so it will not be detected or discovered. The best camouflage for a lie is all the truth that can be associated with the lie. The writer once discovered a lie thus camouflaged by a man who was supposedly begging his way home. He claimed to be hungry and broke when such was not true. He gave his correct age, name, and home address, for I checked his registration card to see. Then after helping him I found that another preacher had just given him several dollars. He had his lie well camouflaged with statements that were one hundred per cent truth. This is the manner of camouflaging that is often and generally employed by false prophets and those preachers whom Satan has out to deceive those who would be saved, or who have an aim and desire to be saved. They preach a lot of scriptural truth, but present a false plan for one's salvation. A gospel that will save one's soul must be the whole truth and nothing but the truth, for thus saith the Word of God.

Before anyone accepts a plan for the salvation of his soul, he should be sure it is absolutely scriptural and that it contains every requirement of God's Word. Partial obedience or adherence to the gospel of Jesus Christ assures no one of eternal life (Matthew 5:25-26). The importance of one's eternal destiny is too serious to trifle with or be careless and indifferent about. Once one has crossed over the great divide, he cannot correct his mistakes or complete his obedience to the gospel. His eternal destiny will be determined by how he lived and obeyed God while on this earth. (See John 5:28-29; Galatians 6:7-8; Hebrews 9:27; 10:26-29.) So make sure you do not go to hell for accepting some camouflaged lie as the only hope of your eternal salvation.

55. Doctrinal Lying

Doctrinal lying is a terrible thing for anyone to contemplate doing; nevertheless, much of it is being done right over the sacred desk and elsewhere, pertaining to the plan of salvation, holy living, and eternal punishment. "I have not sent them, saith the Lord, yet they prophesy a lie in my name" (Jeremiah 27:15). Then we read in I Timothy 4:1-3, "Now the Spirit speaketh expressly, that in the latter times some shall depart from the faith, giving heed to seducing spirits, and doctrines of devils;

speaking lies in hypocrisy; having their conscience seared with a hot iron; forbidding to marry, and commanding to abstain from meats." Thank God, all ministers and professed Christians are not liars, but those who preach and teach things which they know are contrary to the teachings of the Holy Scriptures are doctrinal liars.

There are some rules laid down in the Scriptures to govern and regulate the teaching of doctrines that, if we would always heed and follow, we would never be guilty of telling or preaching doctrinal lies. The first one is that no doctrine is established upon any one, single verse of Scripture. Jesus said, "In the mouth of two or three witnesses every word may be established" (Matthew 18:16). Then we should never teach and preach everything we believe, while we need to believe all we preach. How is this? you say. One can believe things which are not scriptural. Jesus had this to say about what He taught and testified: "Verily, verily [truly, truly], I say unto thee, We speak that we do know [not merely what we believe and think is right], and testify that we have seen" (John 3:11). Be sure you are right before you preach doctrine, as it generally pertains to salvation directly or indirectly and has to do with the eternal destiny of the souls of men and women.

56. Evangelistic and Pastoral Lying

This form of lying could have been dealt with under promissory lying, and was referred to briefly and slightly, if you noticed it; but we prefer singling it out now so we can shoot straight at it. Under this heading, we want to deal definitely with this lying that is done so commonly by quite a few ministers of both of these classes, in reference to their dealings with each other, the churches they serve, and to whom they minister.

Some evangelists never seem to take the second thought about what they promise some pastor or church concerning conducting them a campaign. They receive the request, it is immediately accepted, and they often agree to a certain date for the meeting but never appear on the scene. It costs something to prepare for a meeting as well as it costing something to get to the place. Pastors find that a few disappointments of this nature cause their entire congregations to have no interest in praying for meetings in advance—which is very essential if profitable results are to be derived.

Then there are numerous other evils and harmful results that arise from carelessly postponing meetings or failing to preach them as scheduled. The revival spirit may cool down or the opportune time to reach the people may pass by while the church and pastor wait for the evangelist. Too, they may be kept waiting for the expected evangelist until it is too late to engage or secure one for the summer or certain holiday occasions. Finally, such practices often result in some soul dying lost, who might have heard the gospel and been saved if the meeting had been preached in due time. The points listed are very likely only a few of the hurtful results of this form of lying. There is no telling what one will face at the judgment for it, or will find out to be the complete consequences of such lying.

67

Then, when the scene is reversed and the pastor lies to an evangelist, it also works havoc and hardships here, besides misery and hell hereafter. A good evangelist, who could reach and win hundreds of souls to Christ in a few weeks' time, may be kept idle in this manner while souls go to hell, and he is put on the rocks financially. Pastors, endeavor to keep your word; let your word be your bond in such matters. Do not engage an evangelist for a certain date or season and then call it off for frivolous reasons, or because you have the opportunity to secure a better or more popular evangelist in your estimation. This nature of lying may fit in at a time when it would make the pastor a bit responsible for discouraging an evangelist to the extent that he would quit the ministry and go to work, or even cause him to backslide. Too, it might have a tendency to provoke an evangelist to do some undermining work or hurtful gossip. An evangelist can certainly injure a pastor by informing others of what he has experienced in his dealings with him along this line. The same thing is true when the pastor reports how he has been disappointed and misused by some evangelist. So these types of lying live on, keep producing evil results, and provoke both the pastor and evangelist into doing things that injure the work of the Lord and get them in bad with the great Judge. A lie never dies or stops until it lands someone in hell, if it is not repented of in time. The best thing to do is never to let that swift-winged lie get out of your mouth, as it can seldom be caught once it is clear of your reach.

True enough, there are circumstances that alter cases, and unforeseen things can arise that will keep a person from carrying out his plans or keep him from fulfilling his promises; but there is always something that can be done to adjust matters or make them satisfactory with the other party—whether pastor, church, or evangelist—if one will attend to matters promptly and correctly. A perfect understanding to begin with goes a long way to prevent many disappointments and uncalled-for things to happen. If ministers would always deal with each other with an honest heart and keep in line with the Golden Rule—"Do unto others as ye would have them do unto you"—everything would work out all right and the Lord would be glorified.

Brethren, do not discard the statements of the preceding paragraphs until you have prayerfully considered the truth of the matter, in the fear of the Lord. I write these things in the fear of God—God being my witness. Such practices need to be erased from our ranks, so help us God. The safe stand to take is to always pray about such matters before making definite plans (Proverbs 3:5-6), and then never promise to do anything you do not intend to carry out. When we have promised to do a thing, do our utmost to fulfill it, and by God's help and grace we generally can; for where there is a will to do, there is generally a way provided.

57. Premeditated Lying

This is probably the worst kind of lying regardless of the form or manner in which it is done, and is likely the most damnable of all kinds of lying to the person who is guilty of doing it. One is never guilty of ignorantly lying in this manner. Ananias and his wife lied in this manner. They agreed and planned to lie before they went to church, or the place of worship. This form of lying borders on sinning against the Holy Ghost, and seems to be what Ananias and Sapphira did. Known sin, willfully committed, is one way of [eventually] committing the unpardonable sin. (See Hebrews 10:26-29.) Hence, one had better fear and shun this premeditated lying, or he will [ultimately] doom himself and never find any place of repentance. I do not mean to say that every case of premeditated lying or known sin willfully committed constitutes the unpardonable sin, but there is a possibility of it being thus classed by the Lord. He is the Judge in this matter and the One to decide the case. He does not leave such serious judgment for human beings to decide upon. Anyway, when a person has gone far enough and commits an unpardonable sin, there is no forgiveness for him in this world or in the world to come (Matthew 12:31-32; Numbers 15:30-31). Watch your tongue, not your lying, and always tell the truth if you intend to stay in God's church and make it to heaven. (See Psalm 15:1-2; Revelation 21:27.) One could possibly become guilty before God of lying in this manner, before he ever spoke or acted it. (See Matthew 5:27-28.) Remember, God judges one according to what is in his heart, or according to the condition of his heart (I Samuel 16:7).

58. Tobacco and Snuff Lying

This is a form of lying that is generally found among

professed Christians of various holiness churches or organizations and also committed by children whose parents either forbid them to use snuff or tobacco or desire that they abstain from the use of it. The writer, having pastored a number of churches, has personally discovered that many of the members of the churches of our faith who use tobacco will deny their guilt, when called in question about it, and thereby tell a lie. However, do not understand me to say that all members who take up the tobacco habit, after being saved, will lie about it. Anything that will prompt one to lie should be given some serious consideration, especially by those who desire to make heaven their eternal home. The safest thing to do is to touch not, taste not, handle not.

Since we have added this form of lying to our lengthy list, it is advisable that we explain why a Christian should not use tobacco in any form. First, to be a Christian requires that one be Christ-like. Can you picture the Lord of heaven with a cigar or cigarette in His holy mouth, or with His lips filled with snuff? Then to be called a Christian or to worthily bear that name one needs to depart from all iniquity and filthiness of the flesh. Paul said, "Having therefore these promises, dearly beloved, let us cleanse ourselves from all filthiness of the flesh and spirit, perfecting holiness in the fear of God" [II Corinthians 7:1]. Again Paul informed us, "If any man defile [makes unclean or destroys in any way] the temple of God, him will God destroy [and God has nature so arranged that when anyone partakes of tobacco and snuff that it destroys their stomach, lungs, nerves, etc.]; for the

71

temple of God is holy [and must stay holy if the Holy Ghost continues to abide in it], which temple ye are" [I Corinthians 3:17]. It is the body which is hereby referred to as the temple of God, for we read in I Corinthians 6:19: "What? know ye not that your body is the temple of the Holy Ghost which is in you?" My dear friend and brother or sister, God can give you grace and power to lay aside all filthy habits and be a clean vessel of honor unto His glory. If we ever glorify God in our bodies, as He exhorts us to do, we will have to cleanse ourselves and not partake of any filthy habits of the flesh and spirit.

Many of our precious young girls and women of America are taking up the damnable habit of smoking cigarettes as a matter of social prestige, or to keep pace with the trend and customs of the times. How foolishly and ignorantly they are acting! They are destroying their physical beings, their willpower, their health, their offspring (I Corinthians 3:17; 6:19-20), and in the end, their souls. They are smoking themselves and their offspring out of existence here, and their souls into torment hereafter. (See I Peter 3:11; Romans 8:13.) God have mercy on the rising generations as well as on these smoking men, women, girls, boys, and mothers of today. It seems that man has about come to the place that he is going to commit general or wholesale suicide.

59. Immoral Lying

Just by looking at the title of this form of lying you might be made to wonder just what this kind of lying would constitute, or who might be guilty of so lying. Men and women, boys and girls who commit immoral acts generally endeavor to lie out of their guilt when suspected. Of course, if they happen to be caught in the very act of fornication or adultery, there is no use of their trying to lie out of it. The Bible speaks about wicked and ungodly people adding sin to sin by endeavoring to cover up their meanness and immoral acts. (See Isaiah 30:1.) As the old saying goes: "One sin leads to the committing of another."

Another way people are often tricked into lying along this line is in the case of the putting away of a companion in marriage, a wife or husband as the case maybe. They often lie about the reason for which the former companion was divorced. The case has often been that they did not do the putting away at all; it was their companion in marriage who put them away. All this kind of lying does not keep one from being guilty before God of committing adultery if one remarries for any cause save for fornication ("unchastity," Moffatt and Weymouth). Remember, a mind and desire to commit adultery by remarrying will likely prompt one to lie, and he will have two terrible sins, at the least, to repent of to avoid going to hell. Sin is a dangerous thing to tamper with. There is no end to where it will lead one. One sin is just a steppingstone to another one, often a little worse and more damning than the former. Since there is no sin more damnable to the soul than lying, it is dangerous to commit any sin that might prompt one to lie. Immoral sins of all kind will certainly put one in a position to lie sooner or later, and lie he must, or confess his guilt. . . .

60. Juvenile and Delinquent Lying

It is pitiful to see how delinquent young people will lie, as a general rule. Lying seems to go hand and hand with evil and sin of this nature. It has become so serious until our law-enforcing authorities are very much alarmed over the situation, as well as many others. It is high time that parents and all Christendom become like-wise alarmed, to the extent that they take steps to pre-vent so much of this juvenile delinquency and lying. Children need to be taught by their parents to be truthful and law-abiding citizens. Instead of this, some parents disregard the laws of our country themselves, and lie to and before their children. What less could we expect of children brought up in such environment?

The writer had the opportunity to listen to some offi-cers of the law questioning a young chap of about twelve years of age. That boy could frame lies as fast as they could question him, and if one could have believed his lying story, everything would have been all right. The officers took the boy to jail; later they telephoned and told the pastor, with whom I was staying in Superior, Wisconsin, that the boy broke down under questioning and grilling and told an altogether different story.

One could not keep from feeling suspicious about the boy from the way he talked and acted. The boy had come to the mission hall with his clothes wet, and the pastor had taken him to his home to give him dry clothes and something to eat. Upon becoming suspicious about him, the preacher called the officers to investigate his case. The boy had wandered across several states traveling away from home, if I remember correctly. So on and on the story goes with his case and the case of many others, telling lies and misrepresenting things. This boy never told us one single truth or fact about himself that I can recall to memory. If I remember correctly, he did not give his correct name in full. This poor boy likely learned to lie at home; if not directly from his parents, they possibly failed to endeavor to restrain and correct the evil that they saw was taking possession of him. It is true that most delinquent youths are guilty of lying, and some of them are habitual liars.

Be assured of this one thing, my youthful friend, if you allow yourself to become untruthful about anything, the Lord is going to judge and punish you for your lying the same as elderly people. Any time you have reached the age of accountability, the age or time when you have a mind to determine right from wrong, you are then going to have to give an account of your actions and general conduct to God. The wise man, Solomon, gives you this exhortation: "Rejoice, O young man [or woman], in thy youth; and let thy heart cheer thee in the days of thy youth, and walk in the ways of thine heart [after the things you desire to experience], and in the sight of thine eyes [after the things your eyes lust to see]: but know thou [be assured by this admonition], that for all these things [sins of various kinds and lying] God will bring thee into judgment" [Ecclesiastes 11:9]. Therefore, seeing that this exhortation was given by a very wise man, and is recorded in the Bible, all youth should "remember now thy creator in the days of thy youth, while the evil days come not [before you become a habitual sinner or liar and get fettered with sin to where you cannot free yourself, neither control your appetites and passions], nor the years draw nigh, when thou shalt say, I have no pleasure in them [in being fruitful and serving the Lord]" (Ecclesiastes 12:1). All liars, whether young or old, will have their part in that terrible lake which burns with fire and brimstone (Revelation 21:8).

61. Misdemeanor and Felony Lying

Sin of any nature and of every kind seems to breed lying. If you understand correctly, misdemeanor offenses refer to violations of the law which are punishable by fines, confinement in jail, etc., while felony offenses refer to those subject to greater punishment. So, whether the offense is small or great, we generally find that the offender will lie concerning his guilt and conduct connected therewith. This is what makes it rather hard on an innocent and truthful man when he is suspected in some way of being connected with crime. The law-enforcing officers have learned not to accept any statement as truth until it can be verified in some manner. Therefore, they accuse and disbelieve the innocent man as much as they do the lying offender, until they find him to be truthful and innocent. The innocent and truthful man cannot understand why he is so disbelieved in such cases, due to the fact that he does not understand or take into consideration the officers' viewpoint or experience in dealing with offenders. They must thus deal with all suspects to discover the guilty. The innocent and truthful man will generally have enough evidence to clear himself, and it pays an innocent man to be truthful in such circumstances, for any time an officer detects that a man is lying, he becomes more suspicious of his guilt than before. Therefore we can see that it always pays one to be truthful. The general experience of officers, dealing with those guilty of misdemeanor and felony offenses, is that they find that the offenders generally lie concerning things connected with the case if not about everything questioned.

Then the worst part about this nature of lying is, it will doom that guilty soul to eternal punishment in the world to come, the same as all other lying. It is a much worse punishment than what man can mete out to any offender in fines and capital punishment. The Word of God states that *all* liars will have their portion of punishment in the lake of fire (Revelation 21:8). Just a little more careless drifting down the stream of time and all liars will plunge into the big lake of fire which God originally prepared for the devil and his angels (Matthew 25:41). Man! Woman! Boy! Girl! Stop your lying and make peace with God!

62. Slanderous Lying

Slanderous lying may be defined as that lying which is done to defame someone or to injure by maliciously uttering a false report. While one may tell the truth and be guilty of "speaking evil" of another, he who slanders never tells the truth—always lies. Ill will, hatred, and malice are always the instigators of slander. Jealousy may sometimes be involved. Solomon said, "He that uttereth a slander, is a fool" [Proverbs 10:18], and this is certainly seen to be true when considered in the light of Revelation 21:8, 27 and Psalm 101:5; "Whoso privily slandereth his neighbor, him will I cut off."

The giving out of false reports about someone's conduct, or change of attitude or belief concerning various fundamental doctrines of the New Testament, to defame and strip him of his prestige with the people with whom he is acquainted, is about one of the worst acts of slander that can be referred to. Anything to defame a person, even if it calls for lying, is generally employed by those whose hearts are filled with hatred. "Thou sittest and speakest against thy brother; thou slanderest thine own mother's son. These things hast thou done, and I [the Lord speaking] kept silence; thou thoughtest that I was altogether such an one as thyself: but I will reprove thee, and set them in order before thine eyes. Now consider this, ye that forget God, lest I tear you in pieces, and there be none to deliver" (Psalm 50:20-22).

Slander is one of those debased sins. It debases those who utter it more than it does those against whom it is uttered. Slander generally becomes a boomerang and returns to the one who utters it, possibly in a different form or manner; nevertheless, slander is uttered by lying lips. There is an inevitable law of the holy Scriptures which assures one of reaping what he sows (Galatians 6:7). So he who slanders another is sure to be slandered before he goes very far down the lane of time. Then there follows that reaping, beyond the great divide, that one needs to stay mindful of. It is also certain to follow. (See John 5:28-29; Ecclesiastes 12:13-14; II Corinthians 5:10.)

63. Perjury Lying

Perjury lying is defined in our dictionaries as being a "willful assertion of a fact, made under oath, with knowledge that such (an) assertion is false," or a lie. Many people have lied in this manner and will suffer the tortures of eternal fire in that "flaming abyss"—as referred to in Revelation 20:1-3, 10; 21:8; and Mark 9:43-48—if they do not repent (Luke 13:5; II Peter 3:9) and obey the gospel of Jesus Christ (II Thessalonians 1:7-10), as set forth in Acts 2:38.

64. False Accusations

This accusing people of things they are not guilty of doing is definitely another form of lying. One cannot afford to accuse people of doing something wrong just because they suspect (imagine) they might be guilty or because of some lying gossip that has gotten around to their ears. Such has done much harm in and out of the church, and has even caused some people to lose their lives. It is very easy to get caught in this lying trap.

Church folk and preachers are just as much subjected or exposed to this form of lying as anyone else. Therefore, they need to "be vigilant [keenly watchful and prayerful]; because [their] adversary the devil . . . [is] seeking whom he may devour" (I Peter 5:8)—by getting them to falsely accuse someone. (See Revelation 12:10-12.)

Final Exhortations

The reason some people do not want to receive the Word of God right to the plumb line (Amos 7:7-8) is because they have been living such a loose and careless life as a Christian, and do not care to measure up to God's perfect standard. Nevertheless, God says: "Judgment also will I lay to the line, and righteousness to the plummet: and the hail shall sweep away the refuge of lies, and the waters shall overflow the hiding place. And your covenant with death shall be disannulled, and your agreement with hell shall not stand; when the overflowing scourge shall pass through, then ye shall be trodden down by it" (Isaiah 28:17-18.) We might as well live righteous to the plummet now, for we are going to be thus gauged and squared by the Lord when we appear before Him. (See Matthew 7:13-14; 22:14.) However, in the face of the fact that few will be saved and there are so many ways to sin and lie, those who put their trust wholly in the Lord need not despair—He will take them through.

Too, we need not get hasty, as the psalmist did, because we see that the devil has most people lying in some manner, and say, "All men are liars" (Psalm 116:11). There are some people living who still tell the truth, and if you are one of them, do not be like Elijah in this respect and think you are the only one. God may still have truthful men and women by the thousands—I believe He has, regardless of all the lying that is going on in the world today. We are giving some special information for always telling the truth in chapter 7. Be sure and read that chapter before you lay this book aside.

CHAPTER THREE

Classification of Liars

1. Professional Liars

We include those under this heading who earn their living principally by lying. Probably you never realized that there are some men and women who make lying their principal means of livelihood. All fortunetellers, wizards, magicians, spiritualist mediums, and witches make their living by lying; therefore, such people should be classed as professional liars. Some lawyers, doctors, preachers, shop foremen for garages, and title men could also be included with this class of liars, while there are some men of these professions who are not liars. Please understand that we have not attempted to list all professional liars.

The writer knows of a certain title man—one who

works on securing affidavits, signatures, new deeds, etc., to clear up titles to land and various properties—who drew many dollars a day for his time and thousands of dollars worth of royalties, minerals, and overriding royalties as extra pay for his lying to obtain these things. I heard of him lying to an old man and woman to get them to sign a correction deed, for about seventy-five dollars, which swindled them out of thousands of dollars worth of property. He likely obtained several thousand dollars in tips, or bribery money, for this deal besides his daily or monthly salary. People who could not gather enough courage to lie in such matters would gladly give him bribery money or pay him in handsome wages and bonuses to lie for them, not knowing that they would be a partaker in the punishment God would mete out for such lying some day. Paul warned us not to be a partaker of other men's sins (I Timothy 5:22). Lying is a poor way of making a livelihood, if one will stop and compare the final cost and punishment with what is obtained thereby. Thank God, one can still earn an honest living by telling the truth, if he will only do it.

2. Noted Liars

Noted liars are those people who are known for their lying—have a reputation for their lying. Every child and person in the community or immediate section of the city where they reside knows that they are liars. One dare not repeat what they say or he will become a laughingstock of the entire community. The Cretans of Paul's day were noted liars: "One of themselves, even a prophet of their own, said, The Cretians are always liars" (Titus 1:12). People who have attained or gained a reputation for lying do not have anything to boast of and would be blessed if they should lose or destroy it. A church member who would come under this classification of lying would certainly not exert much influence for any church and the Christian faith.

3. Natural or Habitual Liars

It seems that it is natural for some people to lie, and it is often a lifelong habit with them. David said, "The wicked are estranged from the womb: they go astray as soon as they be born, speaking lies" (Psalm 58:3). Jeremiah seemed to picture the saved from among the Gentile nations by referring to their parents as natural liars and quoted them as saying: "Surely our fathers have inherited lies, vanity, and things wherein there is no profit" [Jeremiah 16:19]. You will notice that these liars lie with ease. They do not seem to be bothered with thinking up lies—lies flow from their lips with such freedom, ease, and speed until one is made to wonder. Liars of this class are becoming so common that many of them feel elated over the fact and often boast of how they can lie. One should avoid lying or rid himself of such practices before he forms a habit of lying, if he is at all accustomed to lying, or he will eventually become a habitual liar. What an awful habit to form, and it is one of the hardest habits to conquer.

4. Popular Liars

The most popular liars that the writer knows of are some of our politicians. They make their lying campaign speeches telling all kinds of lies on their opponents and making all kinds of untrue promises as to what they will do if elected to office—and they receive the popular vote of the town, city, county, state or nation. Tell me they are not popular liars! They obtain some of the most honored and popular positions to be held in our cities, counties, states and nation. David said, "Men of high degree are a lie"—are guilty of lying [Psalm 62:9]. Surely such men would be classed as popular liars. These popular liars are going to face God some of these days for their lying, the same as all others who do not tell the truth. If we only knew it, there might be some liars of this class in some of our churches and holding some high official positions in our denominations and organizations. Those who gain positions in the church or elsewhere and maintain them by lying most assuredly are popular liars, but they are going to lose their popularity one of these days just as Hitler, Mussolini, and others have done. It is amazing to see how some liars have risen to such highly honored positions in our towns, states, nations, and the world and have exercised so much influence and power among the inhabitants of these places.

5. Unpopular Liars

An unpopular liar is one for whom no one has much

respect. Among this class you will find those who gossip, tattle, backbite, criticize everyone, busybodies (those who meddle in everybody's business), and so on. Liars of this kind make a poor showing in all walks of life, but, like all other liars, they too are going to hell for their lying (Revelation 21:8).

6. Lie Peddlers

Fortunetellers and tattlers are all lie peddlers. These fortunetellers go around selling lies that have been printed for years, and tattlers quite often inform their listeners that they could not vouch for the truth of what they are telling. In other words they generally put the lie label on what they are peddling by saying, "I am not sure this is true." Anytime one goes around delivering hearsay news and any of it happens not to be true, they then become lie peddlers. "Keep thyself pure" and stay out of the lie-peddling business if you want to go to heaven when you die. (See Revelation 21:27.)

7. Lie Inventors and Forgers of Lies

Some people are quite gifted and talented in the art of lying and forging lies. They are experts in manufacturing lies, not only to tell them themselves, but for others as well. The psalmist said, "The proud have forged a lie against me" [Psalm 119:69]. He meant by this that they had made one up and told it. Job accused his supposed-to-be friends of being liars of this class. "Ye are

87

forgers of lies," he said (Job 13:4). Some lie inventors produce such marvelous lies that we are amazed about them, just as we were concerning the invention of the radio, airplane, and automobile.

8. Unreasonable Liars

Liars of this kind tell things for the truth that could not have possibly happened. They go beyond all boundaries of reason in their lying and almost everyone, even children, know that they are not telling the truth. There are more liars in this class than one would think, due to the fact that a continual practice or habit of lying finally affects one's mind and causes him to become weak-minded. He becomes such a fool until he believes that everyone accepts his unreasonable lying as the truth. He may even get to the place that he thinks he is telling the truth when he is lying. A person can tell a lie over and over until it will become a truth in his mind. Jeremiah said, "A sword is upon the liars; and they shall dote"— become weak-minded, silly, simple [Jeremiah 50:36]. If you do not want to finish your days upon this earth as a lunatic or spend a vacation in some asylum, you had better not give yourself to lying. There is no question about it, lying has landed many a poor soul in some asylum and finally in hell. Solomon said, "A false witness [who is always a liar] shall not be unpunished, and he that speaketh lies shall not escape" [Proverbs 19:5]. He is going to be punished here and hereafter (Galatians 6:7-8). It was reported several times that the noted liar

Hitler was about to crack up mentally, and likely he was.

9. Lovers of Lies

It is rather shocking to think of one loving lies. However, this is certainly the case with many people today and of past ages, too. There is a bad sense in which one can love the person who tells lies, if he loves him for his lying, regardless of the fact that a Christian should love the souls of all people and pray and hope for them to be saved (I Timothy 2:1-4).

The message to the apostle John from Jesus, as found in Revelation 22:15, states: "For without are dogs, and sorcerers, and whoremongers, and murderers, and idolaters, and whosoever loveth and maketh a lie." Most assuredly you will understand by this quotation that "lovers of lies" are not to be admitted into heaven or the celestial city, and that the Lord has so classed many liars. This classification of liars will include those folk who like to read so-called true-story magazines and books. . . . Those who are not lovers of truth as contained and found in the Holy Scriptures and various religious books and publications generally have a great love for trashy, ungodly, untruthful, soul-damning, and defiling fictitious literature. If one only had the eye and knowledge of God to segregate this class of liars from among the inhabitants of the earth, he might be surprised at the vast number of people he would find guilty of loving lies.

Jesus is seeking a people who love truth and nothing but the truth. They are the only people whom He wants to be associated with for the ceaseless ages of eternity, for He is nothing but truth Himself (John 14:6; 1:17). So it is a case of truth searching for truth and truth-loving people. How will Jesus be able to classify you and me on that great day? Will we be lovers of lies or lovers of truth and the Truth—Jesus? You have something here for thought or meditation, and to help you govern the selection of your reading material and conversations to which you should listen or with which you fall in love.

Some folk like to listen to others tell lies as well as some folk like to read them. The writer remembers how that a number of boys and men in the community where he was reared would gather around a certain liar almost every Sunday morning at church, before time for Sunday school to begin, and amuse themselves by listening to that young man tell lies. He was one of those liars who had lied until he had become silly and almost a half-wit. Supposed-to-be Christians and men of intelligence would laugh at and revel in his lying. All who took part and amused themselves with his lying would have been classified as lovers of lies if the Lord had come at that time, though they were attendees of Sunday school and church. So some lovers of lies are to be found among the regular attendants of church services. They certainly are not Christians and lovers of truth as they should be. So, my dear reader, you had better be careful and never fall in love with anything but the truth and the God of truth—Jesus Christ (John 14:6). If you do not, you will be classified as a lover of lies on that final reckoning day and be assigned to the burning pit.

10. Lie Instructors

This class of liars includes those who teach others how to lie or instruct them to lie. Many lawyers, foremen, parents, and some preachers are to be classed as lie instructors. Abraham was bordering on this when he instructed his wife, Sarah, to tell the Egyptians that she was his sister (Genesis 20:12). Abraham came near losing his wife twice over having her to feign the truth. This might have led to Sarah's personally lying to the Lord, as He stood or sat under a tree near their tent. She laughed when the Lord told Abraham He was going to bless them with a son in their old age, and then denied it when the Lord asked her husband why she had laughed. (See Genesis 18:1-4, 10-15.)

A certain preacher called at the home of one of his members, and a child came to the door and informed him: "Mother said tell you she was not at home." He thereby discovered that he had a lie instructor in his church. What do you think of her as an altar worker or teacher for a Sunday school class? She would have made a poor one if they were not desirous to train children and adults to lie. The writer wonders if some liars of this kind have not worked their way into our altar services where people were seeking a know-so experience with God and a thorough cleansing from all their sins. Such people often instruct the seeker to get up and say he is saved or has received the baptism of the Holy Ghost when he never has spoken a word in other tongues as the Spirit gives the utterance. Some folk go to the altar to get ready for heaven, and liars of this sort prepare them to go to hell, by instructing seekers to lie. Such liars not only send themselves to hell but they sidetrack honest seekers; and if they never get lined up later, to hell they go as a consequence of being misinformed by some lie instructor. Habakkuk [2:18] speaks of "a teacher of lies" and inquires of the profit of such actions. Isaiah [9:15] says, "The prophet that teacheth lies, he is the tail." The devil gets his "tail" around him and drags him down to hell like he did about one-third of the angels of heaven one time. (See Revelation 12:3-4, 9.)

There is a lot of this lie instructing going on these days. One has to watch or others will have him lying so easily—all he has to do is just pass a lie. A certain tire dealer instructed the writer once if he would tell the rationing board supervisor certain things he could obtain two tires immediately, but he could not follow the lie instructor's advice and keep in shape for the place he had started to—heaven (Revelation 21:27). Advice and instructions that will help you make it to heaven are to be appreciated, but this lying advice and instruction is to be refused and disregarded (Psalm 97:10; Amos 5:15).

11. Pulpit Liars

The preacher who employs [deceptive] psychology to get his people to respond in their giving, to cast their vote for him, to attend church regularly, to oust some member, and so on is a liar of this class. When preachers falsely claim to be led of the Lord to do certain things or to preach certain messages, they then become liars.

Then, when they preach to suit their congregations, contrary to sound doctrine as taught and given in the Word of God, to keep receiving their contributions, they lie. Paul referred to preachers of this class in I Timothy 4:1-3 and II Timothy 4:1-4. The Lord had this to say concerning such ministers: "Thou shalt not live; for thou speakest lies in the name of the Lord" (Zechariah 13:3). "Her prophets are light and treacherous persons: her priests [ministers] have polluted the sanctuary, they have done violence to the law"—by their lying [Zephaniah 3:4].

Do not be too discouraged over the fact that there are pulpit liars in the church today. They were in or among the church soon after it was ushered in at Pentecost. The message to the church at Ephesus admitted: "Thou hast tried them which say they are apostles, and are not, and hast found them [to be] liars" (Revelation 2:2). This is one of the devil's schemes to destroy the church, but his tactics, though they appear to be very effective at times, have failed; and the church keeps rolling on regardless of his lying inside or out of the church. Truth and right must win and will win. The gates of hell, with all its lying, cannot prevail against the church to defeat, permanently disgrace, or exterminate it (Matthew 16:18). If you are in the Lord's church, stay in it, and if you are not in it, get in it to stay, for the Lord will oust all liars, and, some day in the near future, bind and put the father of lies in the bottomless pit, along with all other wicked people whom he has deceived with his lying wonders. Remember that all ministers who lie

93

belong to the devil and do not represent God's church. They are false prophets among God's sheep.

CHAPTER FOUR

Reasons Why One Should Not Lie

Lying Defiles and Destroys

Lying defiles and destroys one's veracity and reputation to the extent that it makes him an unfit subject for earth and heaven. We read in Revelation 21:27, "There shall in no wise enter into it [the New Jerusalem] any thing that defileth, neither whatsoever worketh abomination, or maketh a lie." Again we have the words of Jesus: "For out of the heart proceed evil thoughts, murders, adulteries, fornications, thefts, false witness [some more lying], blasphemies: these are the things which defile a man (Matthew 15:19-20). The person who gets into God's church and abides there, and who will eventually make it to heaven, must speak the truth from his heart. (See Psalm 15:1-5.)

Lying Disqualifies One for All Responsible Positions

For a person to be responsible and trustworthy, he must necessarily be truthful. As the title of our section states, lying disqualifies one for all responsible positions, in or out of the church. If lying produced no other results than this one, from a spiritual viewpoint, it would be sufficient to rob one of all honor and rewards here and hereafter. Let not anyone think that he will gain any favors with God by lying. He will rather lose all he has gained, if he has anything to lose. A pastor or leader in the church who will promote one to a responsible position, whom he knows to be untruthful (guilty of lying), is a fool, and he will reap his foolish decision. In fact, lying demotes one in God's sight, and the same should be true with us unless one repents and forsakes such practices. Lying puts one on that downward march to ruin, destruction, and eternal punishment.

My friend, if you are guilty of lying in any form, your face is not set heavenward but is turned toward that awful pit where there is weeping, wailing, and gnashing of teeth. Let me plead with you to repent of this sin and all others and obey the gospel of Jesus Christ, that you might be saved from that horrible pit. (See Luke 13:5; II Peter 3:9; Mark16:15-16; Acts 2:37-38.)

Lying Is Deceptive and Misleading

If you do not want to be guilty of leading someone

astray or be the cause of someone missing heaven, you had better not lie in any manner. Even to lie about there being a Santa Claus might cause some child to be deceived to the extent he would not believe that there is a God, or that the child Jesus was ever born into the world as the Bible informs us. It is an awful thing to deceive or mislead anyone. The blood of such people will be on the guilty one's hands when he stands before the judgment bar of God as surely as he does not repent and obtain forgiveness.

The awfulness of lying is that it often misleads good people, honest-hearted people, people with a desire to do God's will, and puts them on the wrong road to success and heaven. Read the story of the man of God in I Kings 13 and see how a lying prophet (preacher) caused him to disobey God and lose his life, which is typical of us losing our souls. The man referred to in the foregoing chapter certainly must have been a wonderful man of God. His name is not given, but he is referred to fifteen times by this most worthy title: "the man of God." Just think of it, a man like this deceived and misled by a lie! There was a cause for this terrible tragedy, though, on the part of the man of God. He had been plainly and definitely informed by the Lord concerning what he must do, and he should not have listened to or obeyed the false prophet. You and I should measure our lives to the standard given in God's Holy Writ, if we want to make our calling and election sure. What people say about it may sound good and easy, but man did not have anything to do with the mapping out of the plan of salvation, nor can he change it. There is "one lord, one faith, one baptism" (Ephesians 4:5). He who endeavors to get to heaven or to get others there in a different way than what God has planned, is going to make a mess of things and land himself and his followers in the lake that burns with fire and brimstone.

It Causes Many to Lose Their Natural Lives

This was true with the man of God we have just been writing about. The lying prophet did not only get him out of the will and favor of God, but he wound up in the path of the lion that slew him. The lion in that story represents the devil who will get us if we follow lying fables and preachers who do not correctly divide the Word of truth. (See I Peter 5:8.)

Then we have the case of Ananias and his wife, Sapphira, whose lives were taken by the Holy Ghost because of their lying to Peter and the apostles concerning an offering they were giving to the church. (See Acts 5:1-11 for the whole story.) This should almost make the hair stand up on the heads of people who lie in any manner. Especially should this be true of those who have once known God and have been filled with the Holy Ghost, as Ananias and his wife were.

King Ahab is another one in the long list of those who have lost their lives by obeying lying preachers and prophets. Read the complete story as given in I Kings 22:2-38 and note the difference in the predictions of Micaiah, the true prophet of the Lord, and the lying prophets of Ahab. Jehoshaphat, the king of Judah, came near to losing his life in this battle with the Syrians, and many soldiers undoubtedly did, because he and Ahab followed the instructions of those "lying prophets."

About the worst tragedy recorded in the Bible leads back to a lie told by David to a priest at Nob, by the name of Ahimelech, when he was fleeing from Saul. He told Ahimelech that he was on an errand for Saul, when the truth was almost the reverse. David was only lying to him to obtain a sword and something to eat. He later found out, to his astonishment, that his lying had occasioned the death of Ahimelech, eighty-four of the priests of his family, and all the inhabitants of Nob, the city where the priest lived. No history gives any exact information as to the size of Nob, but since it is called a city, we conclude that several thousand people must have lost their lives over this one lie that David told. It is bad enough for one to lose his own life and soul for lying, but when it comes to one's lying causing the death of such a great number of holy men of God and innocent men, women, and children, who possibly never knew or thought of David's telling the priest a lie, it is an awful thing to think about. It seems that the Spirit of God in me wants to cry out to the world: "Stop that lying, mankind, before you destroy yourself and all the inhabitants of the earth!" Many a person has gone to an untimely grave because of some lie being told either by himself or by someone else.

I trust that those who read this book have not occasioned the death of anyone by lying, and that you never will; also that you will not be instrumental in causing anyone to lose his soul by misrepresenting the true plan of salvation. Above all things that one presents or recommends to a person, he should be certain and positive about the correctness of his representation of the gospel of Jesus Christ or the plan of salvation. Be sure you understand it, and better still, be a partaker of it yourself, before you try to present it to someone else (II Timothy 2:6).

Lying Makes One Abominable before God

"These six things doth the Lord hate: yea, seven are an abomination unto him: a proud look, a lying tongue, and hands that shed innocent blood"—Solomon [Proverbs 6:16-17]. God does not want to behold or look upon things that are an abomination in His sight. In fact, He hates such things. This means that He hates a lying tongue; but through His abundant mercy He will forgive and save such a person, if he will repent and forsake such practices. Revelation 21:27 assures us that no liar will ever get inside the pearly gates of the New Jerusalem. When it is summed up, we can see that God does not watch over professed Christians who lie, not to protect, heal, or save them. They are roaming around free and open to the attacks of Satan, who is always on the alert to devour such people.

Lying Is Contagious

Lying is something to be feared, for it is very contagious. Listen to Satan, or anyone possessed by his lying spirit for a few moments, and he will have you lying. Tell lies and you will soon have a host of converts or followers. Parents, foremen, officials, teachers, and preachers who lie need not be surprised to find their children, employees, students, and converts lying too. The whole world needs to be inoculated against this damnable and contagious sin, the sin of lying. We shall later give you God's remedy and serum, which is the only thing that will inoculate one against lying. It is a sure remedy and never fails. It will stop the spreading of lying both in one's own soul and in the soul and lives of others. Some people hate to take it, like many who draw back from the smallpox vaccination, but in the end it pays.

God Hates Lying

Can you see from this paragraph title that it is an awful thing to be guilty of lying? God is not even obligated to chasten one of His children who will lie. Proof of this is seen in the case of Ananias and his wife. Remember, God only chastens those whom He loves. It is good for one's soul to be chastened of the Lord, if necessary, to keep him from wandering too far away from God (Psalm 119:67, 71) and from being lost. If you doubt that God hates lying, just read Proverbs 6:16, 19. In the sense that God loves a cheerful giver, He hates a liar. Is this not reasonable as well as scriptural? Surely one needs to repent of such a sin as this if he wants to find favor in God's sight.

Lying Makes One Like the Devil

Why does lying make one like the devil? Simply because the devil is the father of lies—the one who begets lies (John 8:44). He who commits sin is of the devil (I John 3:8), and he who tells lies is also of the devil. If you want to be like the devil and take on his appearance, just let him help you tell a lie. The devil undoubtedly has many more children than the Lord. Many church members and professors of Christianity, who claim to be God's children and lie every day, are badly deceived if they believe such stuff themselves. All liars are children of the devil and to hell they are going, with him, one of these days. (See Revelation 21:8 with Matthew 25:41.)

God Stands Afar Off from All Liars

This being true, what about the prayers that many people pray who are guilty of lying in some form or other? God is not near enough to them to hear their prayers. Such sin or sins separate one from God by a long way, spiritually speaking. "Remove far from me vanity and lies," said Agur (Proverbs 30:8). What is true concerning this person's desires is true of the Lord. He does not want liars around Him or near Him. The only way a liar can draw nigh to God is by humbling himself, confessing his sin or sins, and forsaking them. (See James 4:8-10; Proverbs 28:13; Isaiah 55:7.) One cannot go on sinning and lying and get near enough to God for God to heal, protect, or guide him, if he never repents. If one is in need of any of these things, he will have to forsake his lying and sinning as God directs and approach Him in a humble manner. The best route is by way of the old-fashioned mourner's bench and by crying out to God until the soul finds mercy at God's holy altar.

CHAPTER FIVE

Some Questions Concerning Lying Answered

Is a Person Ever Justified to Lie?

The commentator who said, "God's Word clearly teaches that no lie is ever justified" was one hundred percent correct, for no lie is ever justified. The Golden Rule— "As ye would that men should do to you, do ye also to them likewise" (Luke 6:31)—excludes all lying to our fellow man. Its equivalent in the Old Testament reads: "These are the things that ye shall do; Speak ye every man the truth to his neighbor; execute the judgment of truth and peace in your gates" (Zechariah 8:16). No one could love his neighbor as himself and lie to him or about him. The Bible demands that all Christians must love their neighbors (Galatians 5:14). "Shall we continue in sin [lying], that grace may abound? God forbid" (Romans 6:1-2).

Does It Ever Pay to Lie?

It may appear to some people that it pays to lie, but in the end it never pays. The apostle Paul informed us, "We can do nothing against the truth" [II Corinthians 13:8]. Solomon said, "A poor man is better than a liar" [Proverbs 19:22]. In other words, if a man could lie and thus become rich, it would pay him to be truthful and remain poor. That is what Solomon meant by his statement. Check on all the liars referred to in the Bible, and you will not find that a single one gained anything by lying. Jacob managed to get his blind father to pronounce a blessing upon him, which was to have been bestowed upon his elder brother; but he had to leave home at once to keep from being killed by his angered brother, and he never saw his precious mother again, dead or alive.

The writer knows of some lawyers who cheated an uneducated man out of about four hundred dollars of mineral rights by lying to him and getting him to sign a deed with one of his sons, who was selling a half interest under the same survey where his father owned minerals. One of these lawyers bought eighty acres of minerals from a man a few days later for four thousand dollars, only to find out that the man did not own what he claimed to possess. The lawyer bought the minerals without taking time to secure an abstract or check the title, as the man had offered to sell for less than what the minerals in that locality were actually selling for. He thought the man was unaware of the advance in the price, while the man was offering them at a reduced rate so he would pay off before examining the title. Anyway, the case proves that it does not pay to lie, even when money is involved. In exchange for the four hundred dollars of minerals the lawyer obtained by lying to the poor man, he lost a thousand for every hundred he had swindled. This is a pretty good answer to our question, "Does it ever pay to lie?" and goes to prove that it never pays to lie.

My father once visited a federal jail and did some personal work among the prisoners, exhorting them to be truthful and confess if they were guilty, assuring them that this was the surest and quickest way out of their troubles. If I remember correctly, there were three persons involved in a certain offense, two women and a man. Two of the prisoners decided to plead guilty while the other one, though she admitted her guilt to my father, refused to plead guilty to the judge or before the court. The judge gave the two who pleaded guilty a suspended sentence and let them go free, while the court convicted the woman who denied her guilt—lied about the facts in the case— and sent her to a federal penitentiary. God is doing the same thing with sinners today. Those who will plead guilty and acknowledge their sins before Him and man, He sets free (I John 1:9), providing they will go on and fully obey the gospel (Proverbs 28:13; Mark 16:15-16); but He gives those who will not confess a lifetime sentence to be served in the lake of fire. It pays to be honest with man and with God and always to tell the truth.

Does a Person Ever Have to Lie?

Some people may think that there are times and circumstances which demand that a person must tell a lie, and the devil may make things appear thus; but he is lying when he tries to get anyone to believe that such is necessary or unavoidable. There is never a circumstance or time when one should lie or must lie. Remember that God has promised to make a way of escape for us in every trying circumstance (I Corinthians 10:13). The writer heard of a man who confessed of being guilty of a penitentiary offense, to get his records cleared up to where God would give him the Holy Ghost. At first he said that he could never afford to confess being guilty of the transgression, but after being assured by his brother that God would undertake for him, he confessed his guilt from the witness chair. When it came time for the judge to charge the jury, he dismissed the case on the grounds that there was no eyewitness to the act, other than the man who did the deed, and the court was not willing to convict him otherwise, he said. So, here is another instance that proves that truth always wins and that one never has to lie about anything.

The writer had a personal experience along this line one time. He was renting some apartments, and during the war one was required to file a report within five days. While he was away for some meetings his wife rented an apartment and forgot to make the report to the governmental rent office. When he returned home, he found that it had been fourteen days since the apartment had been rented and no report had been submitted. The devil suggested to him to report that the tenant had only occupied the place five days, as some time had not been taken by the former tenant, but this could not have been the truth. Upon going to the telephone, he called the manager of the Price Administration Office and related the facts to him. The manager instructed him to file it just as it was and that would be all right, because he was away from home at the time the apartment was rented. The writer almost shouted—and possibly should have—because he had proved the old devil to be a liar. If a man wants to tell the truth and purposes to tell nothing but the truth regardless of how it appears to involve him, God will make a way of escape for him—thank the Lord!

Since all liars are going to be put in the lake of fire with the devil, there is never a time when a Christian or anyone else can afford to tell a lie. God makes no allowance in the Bible for a person to lie under any circumstance. (See Revelation 21:8, 27.)

Who Is Public Liar Number One?

Some men have made some outstanding and terrible achievements in the matter of lying, but the devil still holds the highest (if disreputable) title for lying. No one has ever been able to outdo or outwit the devil when it comes to lying. He is the master performer when he gets on the lying stage. The devil was the one who told the first lie. No one ever knew how to lie until the devil started his lying, but he has many imitators or followers today. It seems that almost the whole world has been enticed to duplicate his practice and art of lying.

How Does the Devil Promote and Encourage Lying?

The devil uses several methods to promote lying, and the best one is by getting people possessed with a lying spirit. You may not know that the devil has lying imps that are particularly trained and given to the work of inducing people to lie. Some of them have specialized along this line of inducing people to lie. (See I Kings 22:19-23.) The devil, in some instances, can even induce preachers to lie. Especially is this true if he can manage to get some of his lying spirits into them. One lying devil had a whole host of false prophets lying to Ahab and Jehoshaphat. About all one has to do to become demon possessed is to yield himself to an evil spirit or to commit unrighteous acts of any kind. (See Romans 6:13, 16.)

Then one of the devil's modern methods of encouraging lying is to put on lying contests and give prizes for the one who tells the worst or biggest lie. These folk who put on these lying contests are certainly some of the devil's most worthy servants, and the Lord is going to let them share the lake of fire with him some of these days, if they continue such practices. (See Revelation 21:8; I Timothy 5:22.)

The devil also uses a great many lie instructors and forgers of lies these days to encourage lying. One has to continually keep on the watch for them. There is no need of anyone not lying because he does not know how and when to lie. The devil will have some of his educated liars tell them just how it is done, or he will even do better than that: he will have one of his lie inventors, "forgers of lies" (Job 13:4), to make up a number of lies, and all one has to do is tell them—he does not have to worry himself about even trying to think up or frame a lie. The devil has lies placed around us like dummies, and all one has to do is pick them up and pass them on to someone else.

Since lying is one of the best and most successful methods by which Satan can deceive and damn souls, he certainly keeps himself and all his imps busy with his lying program. Be careful, or you will be involved before you realize what is happening or what has happened.

Who Never Tells the Truth?

Probably, you have not thought of it or have never had your attention called to the fact that Satan never tells the truth. He has not been known to tell the truth a single time since his fall or rebellion in heaven, since the day he first sinned. (See John 8:44.) He likely deceived one-third of the angels of heaven by lying to them. (See Revelation 12:3-4, 9.) Poor spirits, they are consequently chained in total darkness waiting the day of judgment (Jude 6). There is no telling how many people the devil has deceived by lying to them, or doomed by inducing them to lie.

If you have had the devil talk to you, then you should know that he never tells the truth. The writer has always found him to be a liar. He may sometimes tell some half-truths, but he always manages to get some lying into any information he gives out. When it comes to doing what he promises, he never keeps his word. Do not ever be fool enough to believe anything he tells you. People who lie so much until it seems that they never tell the truth, are certainly possessed with some of the devil's lying spirits and are becoming very much like their father. Jesus had this to say of those who serve the devil: "Ye are of your father the devil, and the lusts of your father ye will do. He . . . abode not in the truth, because there is no truth in him. [I am sure that Jesus knew whereof He spoke.] When he speaketh a lie, he [the devil] speaketh of his own: for he is a liar, and the father [originator] of it" [John 8:44]. Be assured by Jesus that the devil never tells the truth.

Who Never Lies?

The answer to this question might be a threefold one. It can be truthfully said that a faithful witness, a true Christian, and God never lie. (See Proverbs 14:5; I John 3:8-9; Titus 1:2.) With man there always remains the possibility of his falling away from his steadfastness and then committing some sin or telling a lie, but with God all such is impossible. (See Hebrews 6:18.) This being true, how can anyone ever doubt any of God's promises or predictions for the future? Some people seem to doubt that there is a literal, burning hell, but Jesus, who was God manifested in human flesh (Matthew 1:23; II Corinthians 5:19), declared to His audience time and again that there was such a place, "where their worm dieth not, and the fire is not quenched" (Mark 9:42-48; Matthew 25:41-46).

Then, there are others who want to believe and

preach that a person can be saved, during this dispensa-
tion of grace, without being born of water and the Spirit.
If Jesus spoke the truth to Nicodemus, and He most
assuredly did, when He told him he had to be "born
again" before he could see or enter the kingdom of God,
no one is going to get in otherwise. Brothers and friends,
we had just as well face the facts and accept the truth
now while we can and declare the same to others. There
is a great falling away from this truth and message of the
new birth, or the birth that is of water and the Spirit, as
God's plan of entrance into His kingdom. It just cannot
be other than what Jesus gave to us in John 3:3-7, for we
know He did not lie.

Paul said, "Let God be true, but every man a liar"
[Romans 3:4]—that is, if either man or God must be
doubted. To disbelieve God is to make Him a liar, for John,
the beloved, informed us: "He that believeth not God hath
[by such an act] made him a liar" (I John 5:10). To inform
people that you do not believe what they have said is true
is just a mild way of telling them they have lied. Whom are
we going to believe and follow in these days of infidelity
and apostasy? Give me Jesus and His teachings and plenty of God's grace to believe and obey them, for "there is a
way [and possibly many ways] which seemeth right unto
man, but the end thereof are the ways of death" and eternal damnation (Proverbs 14:12).

What Is God's Lie Detector?

The Lord has a lie detector that is more efficient than

113

anything man has ever perfected. While man has perfected a lie detector that works in many cases and is quite accurate, God's never fails and is perfect in its indications and discernment. God's lie detector is nothing more or less than the Holy Ghost (I Corinthians 12:8,10). Read Acts 5:1-11 and see how He revealed the lying of Ananias and Sapphira. He revealed to Peter positively and definitely that these two people were lying about the price they had obtained for their property. God's lie detector does not only reveal or indicate when a person has lied or is guilty of lying but also reveals what he has lied about and all the secrets of his heart. (See Daniel 2:22, 28-29, 47.)

If God's ministers of today would walk with Him as they should, and live where God could and would reveal things to them concerning their congregations, they would be feared and respected more by them, even as the people feared Moses, Joshua, and the apostles. (See Joshua 4:14; Acts 5:1-11.) This was because the people knew by what God was revealing to them that they were the true prophets and servants of the Lord (Joshua 7:16-26). If this were true today, church members and backslidden preachers could not carry on or continue their wicked practices and at the same time profess to be Christians, without being detected and dealt with. We need to make more use of God's lie detector, the gift of discerning of spirits, which reveals every secret of men's hearts by the Spirit, so the devil's works might be made manifest and that lying hypocrites might be afraid to parade their hypocrisy before the church folk and the world.

A minister who does not live close enough to God to know his flock and to discern their spiritual conditions need not expect God to put a holy fear upon the people, to the extent that they will consider his advice and instructions prayerfully and be afraid to dishonor, criticize, judge, revile, undermine, boycott or ignore him. A minister can certainly live where he can see the Lord thus working in his behalf; but he must stay humble, very prayerful, and spiritual, or it will not continue to be his much-prized experience.

CHAPTER SIX

Some Punishments That Await All Liars

1. Stripped of All Honor, Reputation, and Success

We are informed by the Scriptures that "the prophet that teacheth lies, he is the tail" [Isaiah 9:15]. The inevitable consequences of lying make it one of the most serious sins or offenses that one can indulge in or commit. Few people realize the seriousness and danger of lying. One never knows what the outcome of one lie may be until it has taken its course and cut down its victims. A lie is sometimes very long lived—it may die or spend itself out very slowly. A person who is stripped of all honor and reputation, and has had a successful career turned into failure and defeat by lying himself or by being lied upon, is in a pitiful condition. Such people are often left in such despair until they contemplate committing suicide or actually perform the act. Well, these are just some of the consequences and punishments that await those who tell lies. (See Jeremiah 23:30-32.)

2. Lying Causes One to Err

"Thus saith the Lord; For three transgressions of Judah, and for four, I will not turn away the punishment thereof: because they have despised the law of the Lord, and have not kept his commandments, and their lies caused them to err" (Amos 2:4). Who ever lied that did not err? Every person that lies errs from the truth, but there are more ways to err than in this manner. To err also means to miss one's aim, to make a mistake, to go astray morally, to sin, and, in every case, to wander from the truth. When one begins to consider the punishments that await the person who tells lies, he can readily see that such a life or practice never pays off with anything that is good or worthwhile. Well enough, the liar has his payday coming, even if it is sometimes quite delayed (Romans 2:2-9). The worst error of lying is that it certainly diverts one's steps from the path of life to that of eternal death and agony. (See Revelation 21:8, 27.)

3. Lying Causes God to Remove One's Name from the Book of Life

God informed Moses, "Whosoever hath sinned against me, him will I blot out of my book." If there is any sin that would prompt God to take one's name off the

Book of Life, it is the sin of lying; but it is not a question of the degree of sin that is committed—if it is sin, one's name is removed. (See Exodus 32:33 with Psalm 69:27-28.) I suppose that my readers all know what the consequences are of having one's name removed from the Book of Life. It simply means that one's right to eternal life has been canceled and that he must spend eternity with the damned in the lake of fire. (See Revelation 20:15.) There is no chance of being saved for one who dies after God removes his name from the Book of Life, unless he gets God to replace it before he dies.

4. God's Hand Is against All Liars

This alone is a terrible punishment for lying. If God be against us, who can be for us? There is no one who can deliver us out of His hand. The wife may succeed in delivering her child from the hand of her husband who desires to punish him, but there is no one who could succeed in taking anyone out of the hand of God. Too, this means that everything one may try to do is opposed by the Lord. For proof that God's hand is against those who lie, we quote: "Therefore thus saith the Lord God; Because ye have spoken vanity [lies], and seen lies [you received them by way of a vision], therefore, behold [look and see], I am against you, saith the Lord God" (Ezekiel 13:8). Again we read in Jeremiah 23:31-32: "Behold, I am against the prophets, saith the Lord, that use their tongues, and say, He saith. Behold, I am against them that prophesy false dreams . . . and do tell them, and cause my people to err by their lies."

5. God's Sword Is Turned on All Liars

Not only do we find that God's hand is against all those who tell lies, but His sword is unsheathed and turned on them. What an awful and horrible thing to have God turn His sword loose on someone! The Lord cuts to pieces with His sword until there is nothing left of a person. It just simply means utter destruction for the physical man. (See Revelation 19:11-21; 20:7-9; Ezekiel 38:22.) For examples of this kind of punishment, we refer you to Sodom and Gomorrah, the great deluge sent on the antideluvians, the one angel destroying 70,000 with God's sword because David numbered Israel (I Chronicles 21:1-2, 14-17), and the angel that killed 185,000 Assyrians in one night before Jerusalem during Hezekiah's reign (II Chronicles 32:21; II Kings 19:35). These incidents show us how destructive God's sword is and how helpless human beings are when He becomes angry with them. God's sword is drawn on all liars, and if He has not already struck down some liar, He is in the very act of doing so. Possibly some relative, friend, or Christian, standing in the gap pleading with God for that liar, is why God has not already smitten him. (Compare Exodus 32:7-14, 30-34 with Ezekiel 22:30.) Surely, "a sword is upon the liars . . . and they shall be dismayed" (Jeremiah 50:36).

6. Liars Become Silly and Weak-minded

Here we have another list of consequences that are certain to come to the liar, as a matter of punishment for his lying, that many never knew were some of God's chastisements for this sin. Habitual liars become so simpleminded until they actually believe that their listeners believe their unreasonable lying. They tell things that could not possibly have happened and that even a child, whose mind is on the alert for adventurous things and miraculous events, will not accept as truth. One does not have to continue lying very long before he will become simpleminded and silly. If one desires to finish his days upon this earth in this category, and possibly die numbered with the insane, let him keep up that lying or indulge in it continually, and this will be his lot.

To lose one's wit means that he loses that ability or alertness of mind to suddenly and ingeniously assemble and associate ideas and words that are out of the ordinary. In its final stage, it means the loss of the reasoning power and faculty of the mind or senses. A person could go so far along this line until he could scarcely, if at all, comprehend his need of salvation or figure out in any case what would be the best thing for him to do. He would be stripped of all that power and ability to reason out matters and make a good decision. When the devil once has a person well on his way, floating down his lying stream toward the lake of fire, the person seldom has enough mind left to plan his escape or appropriate the means God has provided for his salvation.

Possibly someone is beginning to wonder where the writer has obtained all his information, and if it is scriptural. In Jeremiah 50:36, we read: "A sword is upon the liars; and they shall dote"—become silly, simpleminded, lose their wit, and act and talk foolishly. Then statistics and observation will back us up in this definition. The person whom you find telling unreasonable lies will be found to be quite simpleminded and not very witty, if he has any wit at all. He will also likely be found to talk and act very foolishly and possibly be fickle-minded. People who want to be wise and have a reputation for wit and wisdom had better tell the truth and shun lying all the time. We are informed that to fear the Lord is the beginning of wisdom, and there is more truth in this statement than poetry. Fear God and you will not lie. Why should one not fear God and quit lying or refrain from lying if not already guilty, in the face of these punishments that await the liar?

May God cause all of us to quake and tremble at this message, and may the Holy Spirit bring us before the judgment seat of Christ where we can now judge ourselves and not be judged later (I Corinthians 11:31). We can now judge ourselves and plead guilty—send our sins of lying, and all other kind, on ahead of us to the judgment, and not have them trailing in behind us when we have to stand before that Great White Throne judgment bar of God on that final judgment day. Remember, "a false witness [one who swears lies] shall not be unpunished, and he that speaketh lies shall not escape" [Proverbs 19:5.] My friend, the things we have been telling you about in this chapter concerning the punishment that awaits all liars are certain to come upon them. It is vouched for by God's eternal Word, which shall stand forever, even when and after heaven and earth have passed into oblivion, passed totally out of our memory.

"O God of heaven and earth, who shall deliver and save us from this lying age and generation? We are wretched and undone without you; yea, we are helpless creatures, and without you the devil will in some way or another lead us off into this damnable sin. Be our Deliverer and Savior, we pray. Yea, fill us with that Spirit of truth, the Holy Ghost (John 14:17, 26; 16:13), and so inoculate us until there will be nothing but the truth in us. Then we know that we will not tell any lies. Amen."

7. God Stops All Liars from Witnessing for Him

A liar cannot be a witness for the Lord. All liars are the devil's witnesses, and he must be proud of them. Who could be proud of a liar but the devil? If anyone should be proud of a liar, he would be a fool. David said, "The mouth of them that speak lies shall be stopped" [Psalm 63:11]. It is a very easy matter for God to stop the mouths of His people from witnessing for Him when they begin lying. The control is in His hand, and all He has to do is switch off the inspiration or anointing, as we frequently speak of it. The liar may go on talking or preaching, but he is no more God's witness. No one is a real witness of the Lord who is not inspired or anointed of the Holy Spirit to speak. Our words and sermons must be inspired or given of the Lord for our witnessing to be of Him. No more anointed singing, testifying, preaching, teaching, shouting, or worship for the liar. If the anointing is gone and one realizes the Lord has departed from him, as he did from King Saul, he will do well to look around and see if a lying spirit has not switched the current off. One may lie and act a hypocrite, but that does not at all class him among God's true witnesses. He is a wolf among the sheep, a well without water, a cloud without rain, and a terrible offender in God's sight.

8. Liars Cannot Abide in God's House, Nor in His Sight

"He that worketh deceit [and one has to lie in almost every case to deceive anyone] shall not dwell within my house [church]: he that telleth lies shall not tarry in my sight" (Psalm 101:7). God's house is not one that can be built with mortal hands anymore. It is a spiritual building. (See Ephesians 2:19-21.) Therefore, God can put one out of His building though he still remains in some church or organization. There is a day coming when God is going to cast all liars out of His sight, just as He cast the children of Israel and Judah out of His sight in days of yore (Jeremiah 7:15; 15:1). This might not appear to be a very bad or sore punishment to some now, but wait until they experience it! To be cast out of God's sight does not mean necessarily that one is where God cannot see him, but that he is where he cannot see God or even get a glimpse of Him, His presence, or His power in any form or manner.

We are sometimes relieved of our distress over the loss of loved ones, who have been placed out of our sight beneath the sod of some cemetery, by viewing one of their pictures. There will not likely be any comforting pictures of the crucified Christ hanging on the walls of hell for one to behold. Sinners will be deprived of every vision and likeness of our God and Savior, Jesus Christ. Especially will this be true following the Great White Throne judgment. You, like Paul and other Christians, may have beheld the Lord and His glory in some vision of the night, but if you turn away from Him by lying, you will soon be where you will never see that wonderful and sympathetic face again. Remember, the Lord has said, "He that telleth lies shall not tarry in my sight" [Psalm 101:7], and you may as well expect this if you lie and die guilty of this sin.

9. Finally, Hell!

We have listed in this chapter a great many punishments, though not nearly all of them, that await all liars. There are none of the punishments we have dealt with prior to this paragraph that will or can equal hell, that burning lake of fire that is filled with brimstone and produces an unending experience of death, known as the "second death." When it comes to explaining the tortures of that place with pen or tongue, it is beyond the English vocabulary to supply us with words to describe it—it is just hell, and more of hell, and hell that has no end to it. When one wants to speak of the terribleness of something that he cannot find words to express how awful it is, he just simply says, "It was hell."

In chapter two we dealt with many forms of lying, and

there are surely other ways a person can lie. Surely hell, that indescribable place of torment, must have enlarged her mouth to receive all these multitudes and millions of liars who have been pouring into it for ages past and up to the present time. God told Isaiah, or informed us through this prophet, that He had enlarged hell so much that it was beyond measure (Isaiah 5:14). So hell is going to be large enough to accommodate all liars, we can be assured of that, and that all liars are going there. (See Revelation 21:8; Proverbs 19:5.)

Surely the readers of this book should be ready by this time to consider God's remedy and inoculation for the sin of lying, after having read of the various punishments and consequences that await the liar. So we now pass with you to the final chapter of this book for the much-needed and prized information. Let me plead with you to give the following chapter your most prayerful consideration for your own eternal welfare.

CHAPTER SEVEN

God's Remedy and Inoculation for Lying

The Word of God

The Word of God is certainly to be considered and resorted to if one desires and hopes to free himself from all lying and be truthful in every action and statement. Jesus informed His disciples that they had been cleansed through the Word that He had spoken to them (John 15:3). Then the psalmist said, "Thy word have I hid in mine heart, that I might not sin against thee." [Psalm 119:11]. So there is no question but that there is a cleansing element and an inoculation against lying and all other sins in the Word of God.

A good knowledge of the Scriptures concerning the various punishments and consequences of lying should make any God-fearing person seek the Lord for a greater filling of the Spirit of truth. Too, when one reads and finds that God has barricaded the New Jerusalem and heaven against all liars (Revelation 21:27), and that no one but he who speaks the truth in his heart is going to dwell in God's holy hill (high heaven) and abide in His house (church) (Psalm 15:1-2), he is certainly made to see that one needs to be kept by the power of God at all times and places.

Jesus made use of the Word of God to defeat Satan during one of the archenemy's worst attacks upon Him. What power of resistance He wielded when He said, "It is written"! If the Word of God proved so helpful to our Lord during His sojourn and days of testing here on this earth, it certainly should be read and adhered to, especially by all of God's children. It will certainly help cleanse one from all untruthfulness and play a great part in inoculating him against all lying. "For the word of God is quick, and powerful" ("full of life and power"—Weymouth) (Hebrews 4:12). Read Psalm 1:1-6 and Joshua 1:1-9 and be further enlightened concerning the power and consequences of the written Word, which is assured to those who will constantly meditate upon it, believe it (Hebrews 11:6), and obey it.

The Spirit of Truth

"Howbeit when he, the Spirit of truth, is come, he will guide you into all truth" (John 16:13).

"But ye shall receive power, after that the Holy Ghost is come upon you" (Acts 1:8), which includes power to tell the truth. (See I John 2:27.)

There are two predominating and controlling spirits

in the world, besides our own human spirit, that we have to do with or deal with. One of these spirits predominates to establish truth and righteousness in one's life and conduct, but the other tends to lead man in the other direction, and the evil spirit, known as Satan and the devil, is an outright lying spirit. As we have already explained in chapter five, he never tells the truth. If he gets control and possesses one in any degree, he certainly injects his lying spirit into him. One must stay free from all of Satan's influence and control or he will lie in spite of himself. The human spirit is . . . easily influenced by either of these predominating spirits of good and evil. Therefore, one should see to it that his own spirit is influenced and controlled only by the Spirit of truth, if he desires to always be truthful.

There is no need of man that demands one to be a recipient of the Holy Ghost any more than the one we are now dealing with. Some people, and many of them professed Christians, do not see the need of their seeking God for the baptism of the Holy Ghost and being possessors of this experience today. Without it, it is a matter of impossibility for one always to be as truthful as he should be. The human spirit is not capable of guarding itself to this extent, for it was not created in that capacity. God has created us as dependent beings and not at all independent. Jesus frankly warned His disciples that without Him they could do nothing (John 15:5). The Holy Ghost can be received today, with the evidence of speaking with other tongues as the Spirit gives the utterance, the same as it was received at Pentecost. "For the promise is unto you [Peter's audience on the Day of Pentecost], and to your children, and to all that are afar off, even as many as the Lord our God shall call" (Acts 2:39). (See also Acts 2:1-4, 37-39; 19:1-6.) Millions of people, scattered all over the world and in every nation, have this experience and keeping power in their lives today, as a witness that it is for "all that are afar off," as Peter said.

We shall deal further with this point at the close of this chapter, especially as pertaining to those who have received their baptism in the Holy Ghost.

Faith That Appropriates

One cannot appropriate the promises of God unless he believes that God meant them for him as an individual. "Faith without works is dead," said James, the brother of our Lord [James 2:20]. Then Hebrews 11:6 informs us, "He that cometh to God must believe that he is [that there is a God and that He now lives or exists], and that he is a rewarder of them that diligently seek Him." Jesus also informed us that "all things are possible to him that believeth" [Mark 9:23]. The faith that appropriates is the faith that goes into action—does something about the problem confronted or involved. Our next paragraph will show you and explain what faith in action is, at least in part.

Praying without Ceasing

Just as one cannot obtain things from God without faith, he does not receive them without asking God for

130

them (Matthew 7:7-8), and that day by day. "Ye have not, because ye ask not" (James 4:2). We cannot receive a lifetime supply of spiritual food, power, grace, and so on by praying one prayer, any more than one can eat enough, naturally speaking, to sustain himself indefinitely. This is where "praying without ceasing" comes in. Our spiritual needs must be a matter of daily prayer. "Though our outward man perish, yet the inward man is renewed day by day" [II Corinthians 4:16]. Right here is the secret of why many Christians grow weak spiritually and lose out with God—fail to stay victorious in their daily living for God. They do not "continue in prayer, and watch in the same with thanksgiving," as Paul exhorted the Colossians to do [Colossians 4:2]. The model prayer given by our Lord instructs us to pray: "Give us this day [not some future day or year] our daily bread" [Matthew 6:11].

God has spiritual power and soul vitamins like the manna He served to the children of Israel in the wilderness for forty years. If they gathered a week's or month's supply and kept it for over one day, excepting the Sabbath day, it bred worms and stank. Some lazy Israelites would have preferred gathering enough in one day to have lasted them for many days, but God would not have it that way. The same is true with many well-meaning Christians of today. They would like to obtain enough soul food and power during one prayer to last them indefinitely. God could not afford to arrange things thus, for there would be too much idleness among His people, and an idle soul is soon meddling and into various kinds of mischief.

To "pray without ceasing" does not necessarily mean that one must pray for twenty-four hours a day, but that he must pray daily and continually renew or repeat his petitions to the Lord. Prayer must be a daily routine for every Christian if he expects to obtain the needed grace from the Lord for each day. One who conducts family worship and prayer once a day, or who sees that he gets alone with God in the secret place of prayer every day, prays without ceasing, and you can make this application to all kinds of prayer.

A Purposed Heart

God assures one that he can obtain the things that he desires if he will seek for them with all his heart. Some people are not daily concerned about spiritual matters and their soul's need. If we want to obtain God's favor and help, we must first let Him see that we have a will and purpose of heart to do and accomplish certain things. Daniel purposed in his heart that he would not defile himself with the king's wine and meats, and God saw to it that Daniel did not have to drink the wine or eat the king's meat.

A purposed heart goes a long way in influencing God to grant our petitions. Do not ever forget this. God is not out to waste His time and power upon people who have no purpose of heart. Such a person is like a ship without a rudder or helm—there is no telling which way he may drift or turn. The man who never purposes in his heart to seek God and get right with His Maker will die lost—God will never save such a person. If He did, He would be saving him against his own will. We are free moral agents with the power of choice granted to us by the Lord, and God would contradict His creative plans and actions if He did things for us against our will. This should help you to understand more thoroughly why a purposed heart, concerning telling the truth, is so essential if one wants God to give him grace to always be one hundred percent truthful.

A few quotations from the pen of David will probably add some more emphasis to this thought concerning the need of a purposed heart in the matter of being truthful, or obtaining grace from God to help one be truthful. "I am purposed that my mouth shall not transgress [tell lies, tattle, backbite, judge, criticize]" [Psalm 17:3]. "I said [David speaking], I will take heed to my ways, that I sin not [lie not] with my tongue: I will keep my mouth with a bridle, while the wicked is before me" [Psalm 39:1]. David went to the limit of his ability in purposing not to lie or say things he should not speak. He later learned to petition God's help and assistance in the matter, and I am sure God undertook for him. We find him uttering the following words after he had failed to carry out the purposes of his heart by his own strength and wit: "Set a watch, O Lord, before my mouth; keep the door of my lips" [Psalm 141:3]. Do not overlook the need of petitioning God for assistance along this line, though you desire and purpose to be truthful.

Confess and Correct All Errors and False Statements

This is something that we almost have to force the natural man to do, especially at times when the circumstances are not so inviting. Solomon gave us this

133

admonition concerning our faults and sins: "He that covereth his sins shall not prosper: but whoso confesseth and forsaketh them shall have [obtain] mercy [forgiveness]" [Proverbs 28:13]. Do not say you never lied or that you have always been truthful, and thereby endeavor to cover up your untruthfulness and contradict God's Word. "If we say that we have not sinned [lied at some time or other—remembering that any untruth is a lie], we make him a liar [contradict the Bible]" (I John 1:10). John the beloved also had this to say about confessing our sins and lying: "If we confess our sins, he is faithful and just to forgive us our sins [lying and untruthfulness included], and to cleanse us from all unrighteousness lying" [I John 1:9]. . . .

Save yourselves in this manner from this untoward generation, of which there are not many people who tell the whole truth, and nothing but the truth, all the time. . . . We have to confess all sins, even those that we did not intend to commit [by premeditation]. Sin of this nature has to be cared for the same as the mud, stain, and grease that we get on our natural garments by accident or due to carelessness. Such stains and soiled garments must be cleaned the same as those soiled from wear and perspiration. So is it with our souls. If sin has marred it, there must be an application of the blood before it can be removed.

God demands that we call His attention to these special needs the same as the cleaner does. If we just put a suit or dress in for a general dry cleaning that has some stain and unwashable spots on it without calling the cleaner's attention to it, we cannot blame him if the dress or suit is returned with those spots still showing. God wants us to put our finger right on the spots (confess exactly and definitely) that we desire to be removed from our soul. Too many Christians go in for a dry cleaning spiritually, when they need an overall washing with "fullers' soap" (Malachi 3:2), applied with plenty of water in the name of Jesus Christ. (See Colossians 3:17; Acts 2:38; 4:12; 22:16; I John 5:8.) They can also partake of the Lord's Supper worthily if they have already been baptized in water. (See Hebrews 6:1-3; I Corinthians 10:16; Matthew 26:27-28.)

There are too many "dry cleaning establishments" (churches, if you please) in the land today recommending a cleansing for the soul other than repentance. (See Luke 13:5; Acts 2:37-38; 3:19; 17:30; II Peter 3:9.) Repentance includes the confessing of one's sins to God and whoever he might have personally wronged or affected thereby. These churches also exclude the water and blood bath, which can only be obtained by being immersed or baptized in water in the name of Jesus Christ. The water and the blood are included in the new birth the same as the baptism of the Holy Ghost. (Compare John 3:3-7 with I John 5:8.)

Water baptism in the titles "Father, Son, and Holy Ghost" does not remit or wash away one's sins. It is like washing clothes in water without putting any soap, lye, bleach or bluing in it. One may rub, boil, and rinse all he pleases, but the dirt and stain will not all come out. How careless and indifferent some people are when it comes to seeking cleansing for the soul. The Scriptures plainly and definitely inform us, "Without shedding of blood [there] is no remission" of sin [Hebrews 9:22], and, "Repentance and remission of sins should be preached in his name" (the name of Jesus Christ, Luke 24:47). (See also Acts 2:37-38; 10:43; John 20:31.) Remember, Jesus has informed us that he who tries to get in some way other than what He has planned will not make it any more than a thief would. (Compare John 10:1 and 14:6.) Therefore, confess your sins, if you desire forgiveness and cleansing from them, and be buried in the watery grave by baptism in the name of the Lord Jesus Christ, if you have not thus been baptized.

Live a Spirit-filled Life

We now come to the final paragraphs of this chapter and the whole book. We have been studying the remedy that will rid one of sin and lying in the foregoing paragraphs of this chapter, and now we come to the permanent inoculation against sin and lying. "Greater is he [the Holy Ghost or Holy Spirit] that is in you, than he [the devil or one of his evil spirits] that is in the world" (I John 4:4). There is nothing so important to our being truthful as being filled and staying filled with the Holy Ghost, or the Spirit of truth. (See I John 2:27; John 16:13-14.) The watch that David could only have *before* his mouth (Psalm 141:3), we can now have *in* our souls (John 14:16-20, 26; 15:26), which is nothing less than the Holy Ghost that is evidenced by the speaking with tongues as

He enters into our very soul and body. (See Acts 2:1-4; 10:44-46; 19:1-6; Isaiah 28:11-12; Mark 16:17.)

This Holy Ghost, which is the power and Spirit of God within us, can and will keep us from all evil and sin (Acts 1:8; Jude 20; I Peter 1:1-10) and "is able to keep you from falling, and to present you faultless before the presence of his glory with exceeding joy" (Jude 24). If one will not thus inoculate himself against lying, then he will "fall backward, and be broken, and snared, and taken" by Satan and his lying spirit, as Isaiah prophesied (Isaiah 28:11-13), and in the end he will land in hell (Revelation 21:8). General Booth's prediction concerning twentieth-century Christianity is coming true. He said in part: "I consider that the chief danger that confronts the coming century will be religion without the Holy Ghost," and there is plenty of this kind today.

It is one thing to be filled or get filled with the Spirit and it is another thing to keep filled. Many are filled with the Holy Ghost and do not keep filled with it. One must keep inoculated with the Spirit by staying filled with the Spirit, as Paul exhorted in Ephesians 5:18. It requires as much or more to keep filled with the Holy Ghost as it does to obtain the Spirit. All the expenses of operating an automobile are not dispensed with when one purchases the car. In fact the operating expenses begin after he buys and begins to use or operate the car. It costs a person some of his time and a great deal of devotion to God and His cause to stay filled with the Spirit. One does not sleep out his salvation—it is worked out with much fear and trembling (Philippians 2:12). There has to be a great deal of praying in the Holy Ghost (Jude 20), anointed and inspired praying, for one to stay Spirit filled and inoculated against lying and all forms of sin. The Holy Ghost fills one's soul and keeps the devil and all lying and evil spirits out of him, just as a dental filling keeps the germs out of one's tooth and preserves it.

Some people who attain a Spirit-filled life, fool around and use up their supply without seeking for the refilling (Acts 4:24-31) often enough, and become more sinful and untruthful than they have ever been (II Peter 2:20). But this is not a fault of the Holy Ghost, it is a fault of their own. If there is no gasoline in the tank of a car, there is no power there to make it go. The same is true with a Christian without the Holy Ghost.

May we bow our heads and join in prayer with Jude as we close this message: "Now unto him [Jesus] that is able to keep you from falling, and to present you faultless before the presence of his glory with exceeding joy, to the only wise God our Saviour, be glory [for all the good accomplished by this message or little book] and majesty, dominion and power [in your life and mine], both now and ever." Amen!

B. E. Echols, age 47

B. E. Echols, age 87

About the Author

by Rich Lyons

ELDER B. E. ECHOLS was a well-known Bible teacher, evangelist, pastor, and author during his ministry of 63 years, which began in 1921. He was known for teaching the necessity of being born again of the water and Spirit, and perhaps best noted for his untiring stand for holiness. During his lifetime of 87 years from March 16, 1897, until May 10, 1984, he published countless numbers of tracts and booklets (1,134,000 as of 1945), which were published in 12 languages and sent to virtually every corner of the world.

He was published in many of the Apostolic papers of his day, including *The Witness of God, The Pentecostal*

Witness, The Herald of Truth, The Pentecostal Herald, and *The Pentecostal Fire*. Elder Echols went to his reward in May of 1984, but his works live on in the lives of many people he reached through his pulpit and writing ministries.